CRITICAL ACCLAIM FOR THE FIRST VOLUME IN THE SERIES

Chapter One—On Becoming A Poet

"The reflections of writers such as Jane Hirshfield, David Lehman, Phillip Lopate, and Arthur Sze offer inspiration, companionship, and good advice for any poet seeking permission to embark on their work."
The Writer's Bookshelf, *Poets & Writers Magazine*

"Aspiring poets will find a rich vein of insight in these thoughtful pieces."
Publishers Weekly

"Simply the best collection of essays I've ever read about the urgencies, accidents, experiences, and desires that allow people to emerge as the writers they had never dreamt they might become."
David St. John

"[This anthology] is just smashingly good! I am just so impressed with the density and breadth and solidity of these pieces. In the old days, it would have been one of those books that an entire generation of young poets eagerly snatched for their shelf—I so hope it can still do that now, in these more fractured times. It deserves to be there."
Jane Hirshfield

"Here in abundant variety are clear and often breathtaking insights on the life of art. This brilliant collection will speak to readers and writers alike, to anyone susceptible to beauty."
Brendan Constantine

"Here is a brilliant anthology that is an antidote to that old age advice: Show, don't tell. In *On Becoming a Poet*, twenty-five writers reveal their path to achieving their goals. In other words, they do what we've all been told not to do: they tell, and they tell, and they tell us some more. And in this telling, they offer us the gift of the possibility."
Steve Fellner

QUEST: A WRITER'S JOURNEY

This second volume in Marsh Hawk Press Chapter One anthology series continues to detail and enlarge upon the beginnings and developments of contemporary poets and writers critically praised in the first volume. It is a unique supplement to classroom Creative Writing instruction and to the self-education efforts of poets and writers wishing to explore the possibilities of their craft through the experience of successful older practitioners. In spirit, it represents a venerable and age-old tradition of learning one-to-one from the experiences of established writers.

SUSAN TERRIS Editor

SANDY McINTOSH Series Editor

Quest

A Writer's Journey

CHAPTER ONE SERIES

Marsh Hawk Press · 2025

EAST ROCKAWAY, NEW YORK

Marsh Hawk books are published by Marsh Hawk Press, Inc., a not-for-profit corporation under section 501(c)3 of the United States Internal Revenue Code.

Book Design: Mark Melnick

FIRST EDITION

Library of Congress Cataloging-in-Publication Data
Names: Terris, Susan, editor. | McIntosh, Sandy, 1947- editor.
Title: Quest : a writer's journey / edited by Susan Terris and Sandy McIntosh.
Description: East Rockaway : Marsh Hawk Press, 2025. | Identifiers: LCCN 2024060037
ISBN 9798987617786 (paperback)
Subjects: LCSH: Poetry--Authorship. | Creation (Literary, artistic, etc.)
LCGFT: Essays.
Classification: LCC PN1059.A9 Q47 2025 | DDC 808.1--dc23/eng/20250103
LC record available at https://lccn.loc.gov/2024060037

ISBN 9798987617786

Publication of this title was made possible in part by a regrant awarded and administered by the Community of Literary Magazines and Presses (CLMP). CLMP's NYS regrant programs are made possible by the New York State Council on the Arts with the support of Governor Kathy Hochul and the New York State Legislature.

P.O. Box 206, East Rockaway, N.Y. 11518-0206
mheditor@marshhawkpress.org

Introduction

MY FRIEND VINTY likes to say, "Everyone should do something that makes them feel like they're flying." He's a surfer, so it makes sense. Most days, he is buoyed by a whole ocean, the wind hitting his face. Freedom. And I think he's right—who doesn't want to be reborn a bird? We crave flight in the physical sense and in living a life of expanded imagination.

In this gathering of essays by poets on their evolution as writers, I see words described again and again as a force of the natural world: Forrest Gander on the erogenous language of geology, Xiaoqui Qiu's memory lives on "in the small, delicate fragments of words, like snowflakes in your palm." Jane Hirshfield (quoted by Ellen Bass) describes surprise on the page as "epiphany's first flower."

Language, and what it carries, is elemental, organic, and alive. Here, in this volume, we see how writing can shape a life. Amber Flora Thomas tells us, "I am always thinking about the narrative and how to show a larger story through fragments of memory," and we know we are also being invited to see how this writer has put together a life from fragments. Elaine Equi suggests we might keep a diary of such fragments, pieces of which we might make more, but also pieces that capture something close to our lived experience; the broken, unassembled, incomplete, scuffed bits that make up the whole.

This book reads as a kind of I-Ching for writers. Open to any essay, and there's something to be gleaned about how to hold opposites and cobble together, not only a poem, but a path. David Lehman tells us that we needn't limit ourselves to "one field only, or to one mode within that field." Yes. We can live larger. Denise Duhamel's mentor tells her, "Pay yourself first," in time to write, and we are reminded that art and life require us to choose what we most want. Rusty Morrison says, "I believe I must listen collaboratively to all the selves I am and let them all impact the poem," and we remember that to live fully, you can't leave anything out, can't have the desired without the feared.

Many of us write because we, too, are assembled on the page. These fragments find a home on the page, and we, the writers, find a community. At this moment, when AI is a new and ever-growing aspect of our society, it strikes me that the process of poetry is both democratic and arcane. While the information on craft is widely available on the internet, the story of any given poet—and many of the stories you'll see here—reveals how they've been guided by the poets who came before them, or alongside them. How the art of writing a good line, of putting aside time to write, the resilience to deal with rejections, the will to keep writing in dark times—all are passed down from one poet to another. May this book carry on that tradition, one voice after another, describing, step-by-step, the rocky path down to the open sea.

Danusha Laméris

Online Resources for Students, Instructors and Readers are available at

chapter-one.marshhawkpress.org

Writing Prompts & Insights | Poetic Influences | Poet's Biographies | Videos

Contents

Introduction 7

Jane Hirshfield — *Borge's Generosity & Some Thoughts on Doubt* 13

Forrest Gander — *The Questions We Ask Ourselves: An interview by Jim Natal* 15

Xiaoqiu Qiu — *The Little Dying* 22

Danusha Laméris — *How I Came to Poetry* 26

Steve Fellner — *On Murders, Anorexia, and the Concept of the Soul* 29

Charles A. Matz — *A Shout Before Oblivion: Five Rules* 32

David Lehman — *The Birth of the Best* 36

Patricia Carlin — *At Home* 39

Ilya Kaminsky — *Reading Dante in Ukraine* 42

Rusty Morrison — *Writing into Risk* 46

Denise Duhamel — *In Praise of Colette Inez's "Pay Yourself First"* 48

Tony Trigilio — *The Importance of Being Obstinate* 50

Mary Mackey — *Creativity: Where Poems Begin* 57

Sandy McIntosh — *Coaxing the Hangman* 64

Denise Low	*Gary Snyder and a Lesson in Consistency*	66
Jim Natal	*Oil & Water*	69
Elaine Equi	*Square One*	73
Phillip Lopate	*The Poetry Years*	77
R. L. Stine	*Say yes to things you meet. You don't know where they will lead.*	87

David St. John	*You Can't Judge A Book*	93
Ellen Bass	*Some Thoughts on Juxtaposition in Poetry*	96
Amber Flora Thomas	*A Journey Between Poetry & Art*	105
Spencer Rumsey	*No Spontaneous Bop Prosody!*	109
Eileen R. Tabios	*(Title Below)*	112
Stephen Paul Miller	*The Poetry Mailing List: Poetry Beyond Borders*	115
Liane Strauss	*How to Help Your Non-Poet Friends Enjoy Poetry More (Maybe)*	125

Author Biographies 128

Jane Hirshfield

Forrest Gander

Xiaoqiu Qiu

Danusha Laméris

Steve Fellner

Charles A. Matz

Jane Hirshfield

Borges's Generosity & Some Thoughts on Doubt

A writer sometimes needs encouragement.

THERE ARE, PERHAPS, WRITERS who are sure of their own greatness. Most walk more often—sometimes perennially—in the company of doubt. Awaken in doubt-light, dress in doubt-jeans, wash face in the morning with doubt's cold water and lie down at day's end between doubt's un-warmed sheets: for months on end, the portrait of a working writer.

The best practice is not to engage with the question of one's own work's worth at all—except when revising. While revising, doubt is undoubtedly and boundlessly useful, though even then, a skeptical relationship to what you are doing works best in the service of only one question. That question is not: is this good? It is not: is this bad? It is only: how can this be better?

Writing a first draft is closer to what you do after finding yourself thrown in deep water: you swim. And on the other end of things, when the work—novel, poem, essay, short story—is finished, you don't stand around admiring it or insulting it. You go on to the next, or cook dinner.

Larger doubt—great doubt—is needed. There are times when a writer pauses, feels in awareness some version of the Chinese verse inked onto the wooden block and mallet instrument that announces time in Soto Zen monasteries:

> Life is transient, swiftly passing.
> Wake up! Attend!
> Coming and going matters.
> Do not squander this life.

Great doubt's questioning attention is indispensable to conducting a life unwasted. But small doubt—the doubt of ego and mirror—is useless, a precarity. W. S. Merwin's poem "Berryman" (findable online and worth re-reading in full), ends with a conversation between the undergraduate Merwin and his then-professor:

I asked how can you ever be sure
that what you write is really
any good at all and he said you can't

you can't you can never be sure
you die without knowing
whether anything you wrote was any good
if you have to be sure don't write

"You will die without knowing." The thought is, heard as intended, a liberation and grant of freedom. Writing can only fully unfold in a field of non-weighing, non-judging. You need to take chances to forget your place in the book of existence and make a new one.

Some thoughts of Jorge Luis Borges from the prologue to his last book of poems offer a different mode of escape from self-judgment and doubt:

> After all these years, I have observed that beauty, like happiness, is frequent. A day does not pass when we are not, for an instant, in paradise. There is no poet, however mediocre, who has not written the best line in literature, but also the most miserable ones. Beauty is not the privilege of a few illustrious names. It would be rare if this book did not contain one single secret line worthy of staying with you to the end.
>
> —Jorge Luis Borges, January 9, 1985 (tr. by Willis Barnstone)

People who put words onto paper cannot help but stumble their way into adding to the sum and storehouse of paradise. Borges's generosity, addressed to himself and to all writers, is also a curative, an antidote to self-doubt's silencing grip. Good lines will come, bad lines will come. For either to happen, both must happen; a person who wants to write needs first to be writing. The lines worthy of staying will stay. The others will vanish.

Paper is inexpensive: you can always revise, discard, try something else. Language, too, is generous, its discoveries available and frequent, abundant as wild grass seeds on an unmown hill. Language does not begrudge or judge its own spending. It makes its own newness and carries its world-alterations profligately, freely. Its generative possibilities and stored wisdoms pass through us—our fears, hopes, stories, imaginings, and days—as ordinarily and continuously as life itself does. A thought I find also encouraging.

The Questions We Ask of Ourselves:

An Interview with Forrest Gander by Jim Natal

JIM NATAL: You studied geology as an undergrad at William & Mary and you're still out there exploring the fissures and crevices of the San Andreas Fault. How does Earth Science with its strata, core samples, tectonic plate shifts, and geologic time inform your poetry? Do these concepts and references just show up unannounced like a temblor while you're writing?

FORREST GANDER: Funny you should mention geological fissures. For the last two days, I've been in the Mono Lake area, east of Yosemite National Park. It's worthwhile to look up a photo of Mono Lake online. A terminal lake with white, cauliflower-textured tufa columns towering over its surface, it resembles one of those fantasy landscapes—do you remember the early YES album covers—painted by Roger Dean? In any case, behind and above Mono Lake, my partner and I explored the Black Point Fissures, dramatic canyon-sized slots in an uplifted volcanic dome. Geology helped train my sight. It taught me to correlate large scale features—say, a range of mountains—with small scale features—microscopic views of the crystals in a shear zone, for instance. It takes more than one view to comprehend what you are looking at.

JN: You once mentioned in an interview that the geology of the earth is erotic. How so?

FG: Maybe I said that I think the *language of geology* is erotic. I love the gorgeous textures of geological words: Anglo-Saxon words like slab-gap and cleavage for instance; a Celtic word like crag; blende from the German for dazzle. And, of course, the many Latinate words like ontogeny, subduction, etc. Especially in a time when our lexicon is often reduced to sound bites, quotidian tropes, 280-character tweets, etc., I'm excited by poetry's capacity to expand and renew our language by drawing from a wide range of sources.

JN: Speaking of your college days, one professor in particular did not offer much encouragement for your writing. More than a dozen books, a Pulitzer Prize, and an array of other prestigious awards later, we can safely say you've proven him wrong. Can you explain what it was that made you persist as a writer?

FG: Alas, that professor, Dr. Jenkins, was dead on. I thought I was a hot-shot poet in my freshman year at William & Mary, but I hadn't been reading much contemporary poetry beyond Dylan Thomas and Carl Sandburg. After David Jenkins' honest, withering critique, I started voraciously reading contemporary poetry, and I signed up for a poetry workshop taught by Peter Klappert, a Yale Younger Poets Prize winner. He was the first living poet I'd met, and his seriousness about the art was influential. But you never really know about the quality of your work, do you? The prizes aren't necessarily indicative of anything but moments of good luck. Emily Dickinson and Gerard Manley Hopkins went unrecognized and unrewarded in their time. Longfellow was the most popular poet in the English-speaking world for a while. Robinson Jeffers appeared on the cover of *Time* magazine and was lionized in portraits and busts by dozens of major sculptors and photographers. Few people read Longfellow or Jeffers anymore (although I do re-read and admire Jeffers' work). You don't know. You struggle on. I try not to repeat myself. I imagine every artist thinks, like me, that their *next* work is going to outshine anything they've done before. For me, it's the shrapnel of hope more than faith or assurance that drives me.

JN: During the conversation portion of a Lannan Foundation program you did with your close friend, poet Arthur Sze, you say that asking "Why not?" is the "beginning of all good art." What "why not" questions have you asked yourself as your literary career has progressed?

FG: Why not incorporate vocabulary from nontraditional sources like geology or physics into poetry? Why not risk writing about encounters with the foreign? There are serious aesthetic and ethical reasons, in both those cases, for why it might be better *not* to go there. In *Mojave Ghost*, my new book, maybe I come close to formulating my reasons for taking those risks when I write, "Only when we reach the edges of experience/ do we begin to intuit the more-than-this."

JN: With your late wife, the poet C. D. Wright, you were co-editor of Lost Roads Publishers. With the recent closure of a mainstay small press distributor and the burgeoning squeeze—particularly on new writers—to print and distribute their work through Amazon, plus the consolidation of major publishing houses internationally, what do you see as the future of independent publishing?

FG: What's the future of *any* book publishing? Are most of the major New York publishing houses, as they dump their older editors, also weaning themselves of "the literary" in order to score bigger markets? Will there be books in fifty years? My son, in his mid-thirties, thinks not. A headline in *The New York Times* this morning announces "A.I. Can Write Poetry, but It Struggles with Math." I'm no good with predictions. I'm devoted to something that has value to me, whether or not there is a place for it in our rapidly changing culture. I know others who feel the same way. Maybe the fact that poetry has, for the most part, always existed outside the market economy bodes well for its place in the future. I think there will always be people who consider poetry—written by people—important, even critical to human experience. In an interview, Raúl Zurita once said to me, "Because it is what opposes death, poetry is the hope of what has no hope. It is the possibility of what has absolutely no possibility. It is the love of what has no love. Like death, poetry was born with the human and will die when the last of our kind contemplates the last sunset."

JN: *Mojave Ghost,* your new book, is difficult to categorize. You subtitle it a "A Novel Poem" and it is that on many levels and shades of meaning. It's a book-length poem that has a novel-like arc and a narrative, discursive style. And it has a novel (as in unusual) fragmentary, short chapter structure. How did you decide to present this material in such a way? What freedoms—or restrictions—did it grant?

FG: Like you, I've been open to formal changes in my work. In *Mojave Ghost,* I wanted to write about the complexities of intimacy in the most direct way possible, without the lyricism, the energized and counterpointed music of my recent books. I've felt devastated by the successive recent deaths of my wife, C. D. Wright, my mother (who raised me and my sisters by herself), and my younger sister with whom I was inordinately close. Those deaths have shattered me and staggered my thinking, my feeling, my language. I found I could only write in fragments, in stages, stutters. But at the same time that I began this book, I fell into a profound, loving relationship, now a marriage, with the sculptor Ashwini Bhat. But my happiness was torn open by my grief. My consciousness felt ripped into a present and a past that I couldn't distinguish from each other. I started to speak to and experience myself in the second and third person. Our country is increasingly divided politically. Having moved back to California where I'd been born and where I've been trying to ground myself in the landscape again, I began, with nonstrategic and nonliterary intentions, to hike along the length of the San Andreas fault. All those churning, contrary forces reshaped me and my writing.

JN: The book also is an unabashed love letter to your beloved intertwined with reflections on your relationship and your signature keen natural observations, many dealing with the *Mojave Desert* environment where you were born. The desert can be a place of exile and wandering, a spare landscape where mystics and prophets seek enlightenment or are tested. In *Mojave Ghost* it serves as a place to reassess, to question oneself under the glare of the sun. You write: "When you go still, what has disappeared comes forward." Is being in nature meditation for you?

FG: Yes. And I'd note that your own work also often counterpoints the nonhuman world with the technological and constructed world.

JN: Also threading through the book's fragments, the connective veins so to speak, is an ongoing dialectical self-examination, a confrontation with what you've called "the skip at the center of ourselves." Is *Mojave Ghost* a summing-up or more a state-of-the-self report?

FG: A "state-of-the-self report"? Yes, if the self is considered to be—as it is in your books too—the complex of our intimate engagements with others, and with place, and with the multiple selves that compose and complicate what we call our own identities.

JN: To continue on a similar track, a recurring theme in your work is the meaning of a well-lived life. Reminiscent of Rilke's "You must change your life" and James Wright's "I have wasted my life," in *Mojave Ghost*, your childhood self asks, "What have you done with your life?"; your adult self later questions, "How do you answer for your existence?" This echoes what you previously posed in the poem "What it Sounds Like" from your collection *Be With*: "You who were given a life, what did you make of it?" Are these questions that the living can truly—or fully—answer?

FG: I guess I think that when anyone—scientist, poet, stevedore, or philosopher—thinks they have truly and fully answered that question, or really any question, they only show that they have little sense of history. Of their own history or the history of the world's so-called truths. And yet the questions we ask of ourselves are precisely what orient us toward the meaning of our lives.

JN: Along with your own much-lauded poetry, you are an esteemed translator of global poets, including Pablo Neruda. You've called the act of translation "The deepest kind of reading and also the deepest kind of listening to the music in someone else's mind." You also quote jazz legend Miles Davis, who maintained: "You have to listen *into*, not *to*." What was your impetus to translate the work of poets from other cultures? Why do you think their voices need to be shared with what you've termed "an American ear and audience"?

FG: There's of course a rich body of literature that we inherit as speakers of English. And then there's another reservoir of capital, the coin that enables us to travel across borders. I would be impoverished had I never been able to read contemporaries such as Laszlo Krasznahorkai (in Ottilie Mulzet's translation) or Inger Christensen (in Susanna Nied's translation) or Clarice Lispector (in Idra Novey's translation). The first book I fell in love with was a child's book of fairy tales from different cultures. And when I've been utterly knocked out by great writing in the Spanish language—Jaime Saenz, Coral Bracho, Antonio Gamoneda, Zurita—I've felt driven to champion that work to others in my own translations. It's commonly noted that the percentage of books in translation in the United States is much smaller than in other countries, and that fact may speak to a sense of self-satisfaction that I've never felt. Throughout history, English has been enlivened and transformed by translations. They refresh the gene pool of our language. On a selfish level, perhaps, I've always wanted to know what's going on in my art in other places.

JN: You've translated poets whose work embodies disparate poetic traditions. And you've written extensively about the art, process, and challenges of translation. How has your translation work affected or influenced your own poetry?

FG: The influence has been considerable. There's no closer kind of reading than in the act of translation when you hope to come as near as possible to hearing the music of someone else's mind. That sort of highly intensive attunement can heighten your fluency with syntactical, lexical, imagistic, and rhythmic techniques that weren't a part of your own poetics. So while translating, your own wingspan often broadens. It's sometimes the poets most distinct from you who have the most to offer you. For instance, in translating the work of Gozo Yoshimasu, I came to appreciate experientially how his poems function more as core samples—studies in depth—than, say, landscapes. Rather than unfolding horizontally like stories and generating accumulative rhythms, Gozo's poems keep drilling down through his starting material. Instead of writing "I met a cinematographer, and we walked to the river," he'll consider that it's ethically important to qualify every term. Who is "I" and what was "I" doing earlier that day? What kind of mood was "I" in? Where did the meeting take place, in what month, at what precise time? What associations with that particular place does the poet keep in mind? What kind of regard does the speaker have for the cinematographer? Etc. The poem builds vertical volume instead of span or traditional plot. This slows the pacing down, which is a risky thing to do. But it's a risk that can bring unusual rewards.

Translating Mexican poet Coral Bracho, on the other hand, helped to teach me how to trust and to lean more often on musical rather than semantic meanings. Although I have mono-focus and can only work on one thing at a time, either a translation or my own writing, the two constantly inflect on each other.

JN: Translation is collaboration between you and the poet you're translating as well as with your co-translators. You're also involved in a number of interdisciplinary collaborations. What is the appeal of such collaborations?

FG: As a lifelong endeavor, I continue to collaborate with artists from other mediums. For me, collaboration models a social mode—cooperation, mutual inspiration, a release of the need for total control, and orientation by process—to which I aspire. I've always been drawn—as an admirer—to other arts. Most recently, I've collaborated with the Swiss-American photographer Lukas Felzmann on a book titled *Across Ground.* He took photographs of the ground in all fifty-eight counties of California. In the short poems I wrote for each photograph, I respond to the images and also to the geology and topography of the locality. In some ways, this book is just the opposite of my recent collaboration with

Jack Shear in the book *Knot*. In Jack's photographs, there is only the naked human body wrestling with a large black cloth in a place with no background, no landscape. In a separate project related to my collaboration with Felzmann's photographs of California's ground, I've been hiking along the eight-hundred-mile length of the San Andreas fault with Ashwini Bhat. In Los Angeles, the Shoshana Wayne gallery curated one exhibition, "In Your Arms I'm Radiant," of this ongoing collaboration featuring Bhat's sculptures and my text.

JN: So much of your work is in dialogue with nature, infused with natural references; you've even written a poem in the voice of lichen. In the final section of *Mojave Ghost*, you dangle your feet over a fissure of an earthquake fault. You've commented that the San Andreas Fault is a perfect metaphor for poetry in our time.

FG: Yes, I've been focused—by inclination—on environmental and ecological concerns throughout my life. I grew up in a time of major ecological crisis and my concerns, since childhood, have often been focused on the relationship between the human and the non-human. With regard to the San Andreas Fault, I think I said that I've been thinking of it as a metaphor not necessarily for the poetry of our time, but for our time (and my poetry). The tumultuous political divisions that define the United States and many other countries now, the rift between artificial intelligence and human intelligence, the reflexive philosophical and religious assumptions regarding the privileged place of human beings relative to everything else have, together, created a shear zone, a troubled and dangerous fricative landscape akin to an enormous fault running through our world. In my case, I have to add my own subjective experience of rift—between grief and happiness, between the presence of the living and the presence of the dead, and between the multiple selves that constantly argue over who I am.

Xiaoqiu Qiu

The Little Dying

WHEN MY GRANDFATHER on my father's side passed away in 2018, I had just arrived in the U.S. for my second stint of grad school. I learned about his passing from a text message from my mom on the other side of the Pacific. I was driving through the desert with my friends and saw all the red rocks which belonged to an age called Great Dying 250 million years ago when all life on earth almost died out—the greatest extinction event that ever happened on this planet. I dined at a roadside restaurant in a town dubbed "the biggest small town in the U.S.," and watched the car lights twinkle in the mauve Arizona sunset that looked like a failed apocalypse. I felt nothing. I searched the interior of the restaurant trying to materialize my unnamable feeling. And all I found was ketchups: Ketchup-colored booths, Ketchup-colored desks, Ketchup on the desks, Ketchup-colored counters, and waitress with Ketchup-colored aprons . . . I watched a middle-aged man putting Ketchup on his scrambled egg next to a poster of a fishing contest on which a tuna opened its eyes wide in a shade of Ketchup. And I realized I had nowhere to begin to mourn—nothing here reminded me of home.

Then a certain phrase fell out of my tongue. "zen-ya-vu-tan." I heard myself say. It is a term to express seeing strange and incomprehensible things in Wu Chinese, the largest language in the world that is not recognized officially. It was a bit surprising, or even jarring, for me to hear it for I had been immersed in English, willingly or unwillingly, for the past month trying to acclimate myself. I pressed my mind upon this word, trying to hold onto it a second longer, like observing a dandelion caught on my sweater in the wind, wondering from which distant lost paradise it has been sent. Then I had it. It was grandpa who first "taught" me this word—he didn't "teach" me the word: he used it, and I understood it contextually. At the time, I just thought it was a funny-sounding word and somehow collected it in my heart like a strange conch shell on the beach in my half-wet pocket. I didn't find out which four Chinese characters until years later.

It was the last day of my mom's career. I was helping my mom clean her office, which she occupied for more than thirty years. Thirty years she worked and toiled in her classrooms tirelessly and made this small high school's name a household one in the province. And yet the school denied her delay retirement for financial reasons. I watched the chromatic book spines taken down from her shelf and imagined the iridescent plumages of guacamayas flying off to the setting sun in the noise of quick and unthinking saws. I caught one falling. It was a marooned covered book titled "Record of Dirt-Tongues." Dirt Tongues is a colloquial term for the Wu Chinese variant of my town, a language, like many of the other hundreds of "Fang Yan" or regionalects in China, which does not have official recognition and is considered "uncivilized" compared to standard Mandarin.

Yet, linguistically, many of them (Cantonese, a dialect of Yue Chinese, for example) are as different from Mandarin than Spanish is from French. I recalled briefly reading a news piece that predicted "Dirt Tongues" were going to die out in thirty years as I listened to my mom talking on her phone in her accented Mandarin. She still couldn't curl up her tongues or nasalize her "ing's as she was supposed to in standard Mandarin, but that did not stop her from comforting and encouraging countless young hearts to be what they wanted to be during the last thirty years. (Inside the classroom, only Mandarin is allowed.) Perhaps times change, and the next thirty, indeed, will be different. I cradled the book in my arms as I watched as another unmarked and unnamed cardboard box was taken down to the truck. The office looked quite different now. But I couldn't point to exactly when, on that midsummer afternoon with the sun lavishly shining through the windows and sprinkled on the desks like gilded brocades, it started to change. It was one book at a time, one box at a time, one small memorabilia at a time, that the office got rid of the very last trace of its owner who dwelled there for over ten thousand days.

In the bumpy truck, which my dad borrowed from my uncle for the day that boasted a 2000's Japanese AC system, I found out the four corresponding characters of that phrase indicating strangeness: it literally means "households of fairies and wild gods." How fitting and rich in meaning, I thought. I flipped through the remaining pages of the dusty book, which had been collected and compiled by an old friend of my mother, who travelled through the local villages talking to the oldest generations who could remember. And I saw visions. I heard voices. I heard my great-grandpa speaking: that one time when I was seven and he came to visit us for Mid-Autumn Festival. He pointed at the convoluted arteries on his leg that looked like curled up pothos stalks and told us all about his time paddling on the waterwheel under the unforgiving sun and even less forgiving whips of warlords in the Republic of China; I heard the voices of my grandma on my mother's side who told me about how she gathered tree bark and hid it in a wine jar from the starving neighbors to survive the great famine that took the lives of thirty million; and I heard my grandpa's speech with winds from the rice-fields leaking through his teeth the time he put a red armband on his sleeve and led the Red Guards storming the Buddhist temple of the village, but hid the statues underground, shovel by shovel . . . lastly, I heard my nephew last week when he boasted about finishing top in school and ranked 1 in the mobile game *Honor of Kings* on his iPhone X in impeccable Mandarin to answer the queries of three other relatives that asked him in "Dirt-Tongue."

And I blinked my spellbound eyes at the sirloin beef just served in this Arizona restaurant. In the steam, something rushed open my blood vessels, and flew torrentially like the the toppled Pacific and Atlantic in the aftermath of a meteor that hit Chicxulub 65 million years ago in the Mexican coast. They live on. They live on. Not as an entirety of physique, a collection of memories, or a lifetime of existences—but as small, delicate fragments of words, like snowflakes in your palm, ticklish but coldless, and melt in you when you press your warmth upon them. And when they die, they die unceremoniously and soundlessly, in bits and pieces, rather than in the explosive spectacle that extinction usually promises. This is what makes it dangerous, because its pain is almost always felt afterwards, in strange, distant places where the source of the suffering is muffled by the thickness of time and distance. There is nothing more tragic than this moment when, somewhere deep down, a profound and nascent cry of pain starts to form but stops right at your throat.

So, I start to walk forward by walking backwards. To peruse every little dying along the way that proves me alive, and my ancestors living in me, too. I make my eyes spellbound on every new thing I see as if only by the apparitional shadows of my former life that the present is adumbrated with meaning. It is a Celtic myth that when one dies, this memory would be stored in otherworldly objects, retrievable only by visions. I would go on to live in America for another seven years, and the idea of home only stayed alive because it died a little each time I pressed my tongue upon it.

Danusha Laméris

How I Came To Poetry

THE THING ABOUT BEGINNINGS, is that there are so many points along the arc of time to choose from. One story begins with me as a girl on Dover Beach, Barbados, walking in the white sand and listening to my grandfather, Gordon Bell, and his friends recite poems aloud as they strolled, men with names like Nealton Seal and Bruce St. John, men I later found listed in anthologies of Caribbean writers. The sound of their voices lifted on the breeze. Whatever music carried them, I wanted to carry me.

Or maybe it begins in the carpool lane, crossing the Bay Bridge to San Francisco, my mother at the wheel reciting Tennyson as she drove my brother and me in the mustard yellow station wagon I hated.

> At noon the wild bee hummeth
> About the moss'd headstone:
> At midnight the moon cometh,
> And looketh down alone.

She might say, stalled in rush hour traffic, evidence of her once photographic memory and British education. She could recall anything she'd read before the age of sixteen as though seeing it on the written page.

I'm not sure how it happens to any of us, or how it happened to me. To end up in a life of writing is, as I see it, a tremendous privilege. A vocation that sounds akin to "I make a living blowing soap bubbles." Wispy, intangible.

And yet it has been a thing of almost tensile strength, the frame of the house in which I have lived all these years, even as so much else has given way.

I'd been a kid shuffled back and forth between a tense household in Berkeley with my mom and stepdad, and my father, who was prone to drinking and fits of rage, and who, facing divorce from my mother, kidnapped my brother and me from school one day, taking us out of state into hiding for the better part of a year.

I mean to say that, by age seven, I'd seen some things. After that, we lived with him on the Lost Coast of California every summer and winter vacation, in an unfinished house that leaked when it rained. Some days, I was tasked with making sure my brother and I were fed, finding money on the floor around the house, and walking my then four-year old sibling to the campground to buy eggs and cheese and bread.

I was caught between worlds: A life of private schools and trips to museums and plays, and this other wild and lonely life on the coast. Neither a place I felt safe, rooted, at ease.

When I learned to write, I felt something shift. A new power came over me. I remember telling my mother, after I wrote a school report on Harriet Tubman, that I was going to be a writer when I grew up. The report was bound in a purple paper folder with a waxy finish. I thought I'd written the quintessential guide to Ms. Tubman and might be called to present on PBS at any minute. In short, I was proud.

And then there was Alice Simon, the bespeckled, bicycle-riding English teacher who taught sixth grade. In her keeping, we read Steinbeck's *The Red Pony*, which I loved, and at the end of the year, she bound all my writing together and handed it back to me, tied up in a pink, satin bow.

In high school, Mr. Ward, arguably the school's sternest and most effective teacher, (appropriately, he also taught Aikido), took me aside and suggested that writing might be something I take seriously. I came to welcome the notes he scrawled in red on my papers, the way he pushed me to think harder, say more, take risks.

In my senior year, the poet Tony Hoagland, his first chapbook out, was dating Betty, the Spanish teacher. He offered a one-week class for about five of us, and we loved it so much it turned into a summer of poetry. We paid him some small fee to continue to teach us in his one-bedroom apartment in North Berkeley. He read us Rilke and had us write poems and then share them in group. It was heaven. I couldn't write a poem, but I loved trying.

In college, I studied painting at the foot of the Santa Cruz mountains in California. Immersed in watercolors and oils, I was happy staring out a window and down at the vast fields of wildflowers to the sea. Looking at the world through the lenses of color and light, I almost didn't care what I was observing, as long as I could study its shadows, see the hidden hints of green, the dappled purple. An unexpected tinge of umber.

And then one day, I saw a flyer for a writing group with Ellen Bass and felt an urge to give it a try. I spent years there, meeting weekly in Ellen's living room, taking in the nuts and bolts of writing as the wind moved in the limbs of the olive tree outside her living room window. Sometimes, the poets Dorianne Laux and Joseph Millar would come visit and I'd be invited to write with all of them at ten in the morning, getting the day off to a fine start. When I attended the Community of Writers Conference, Lucille Clifton invited me to lunch every day for a week, sharing intimacies and family photos, and telling me funny anecdotes about her life in poetry. Somehow, I had entered into a kinship with poetry and with poets.

I now believe we know who we are, in large part, by knowing who and what we belong to. And I belonged here in the world of poetry. The world foreshadowed on my grandfather's breath, dissolving into the breeze, in my mother's recitations at rush hour. In the pages of the early books I loved, and in the hands of teachers who opened those books to me. Sometimes, looking back over the winding path that has brought me here, I like to say that poetry—and poets—have raised me. And they have. And do. Every day.

Steve Fellner

On Murderers, Anorexia, and the Concept of the Soul

NEVER ASK A POET, "Who made the greatest impact on your writing?" They'll always do the same thing; they'll hem and haw and then say, "There's so many. I could never choose *just* one."

This is a respectable answer.

Perhaps I'm not respectable: I can offer *just* one. I don't even need to think about it. No doubt, no second guessing. No matter how much I reflect, my answer never changes.

Frank Bidart. Frank Bidart. Frank Bidart.

Chiefly known for his dramatic monologues, Bidart deals with people who are in the most extreme circumstances. Perhaps his most famous poem is "Herbert White," written in the voice of the title character, a real-life child murderer and necrophiliac. You can imagine the knee-jerk criticism: he's sensationalizing this monster, which is sort of understandable, even if wholly reductive, especially with Bidart's poetic acuity.

When the remake of "Halloween" came out, I was upset at how they handled the characterization of Michael Myers. In the original, Myers is an opaque presence: we never understand exactly what made him evil. In the remake, the director has the audacity to explain it. He turns the fun of witnessing evil into a cinematic advocacy for pathology: bad childhood, etc., etc. Bidart rarely resorts to a simple determinism.

But even more than "Herbert White," Bidart's poem "Ellen West" has proven to be the most impactful on my writing. West was an actual woman who suffered from anorexia. She lived from 1888-1921. Dr. Ludwig Binswanger used her as a vehicle to articulate the need for existential psychology: the understanding of a person in a more complicated, human/humane way than what mere science could provide. You could say that Bidart's genius is to use this theory as a way of exploring the connection between form and content in the personae poem.

It may at first seem surprising that the most sophisticated poem about a woman dealing with an eating disorder was written by a gay man. (I'd award second place to Denise Duhamel's poem "Bulimia.") But when you think of how gay men cross-identify with women, and the fact that both groups are subject to the male gaze, it begins to make sense. Everyone wants to look good for the heterosexual father figure. Patriarchy makes demands on everyone's body. I don't want to go on at length about this. If one does, you make "Ellen West" seem like a remedial text in a Women's Studies 101 class.

Look at the awesome opening section of "Ellen West":

I love sweets,—
heaven
would be dying on a bed of vanilla ice cream . . .

But my true self
is thin, all profile

and effortless gestures, the sort of blond
elegant girl whose
                                        body is the image of her soul.

–My doctors tell me I must give up
this ideal;
        but I
            WILL NOT . . . cannot.

Only to my husband I'm not simply a "case."
But he is a fool. He married
meat, and thought it was a wife.

I don't want to say that Ellen West's voice is musical. But in a poem that consists of thirteen sections, all varying lengths, there are definite crescendos and atonalities that binds us to this strange, exasperating, appealing, self-aggrandizing Ellen West. You could say it's operatic, but then again, that implies all artifice, which would be disrespectful to Bidart's success and Ellen West herself.

After I graduated with a PhD, I wanted a career teaching poetry. But even then, twenty years ago, the jobs had all dried up. You had to have a book from a major press. I was nowhere near that. But it was still possible to get one in creative non-fiction. They had just started using that annoying label (along with the even more annoying "cross-genre"). I searched for touchstones in magazines, but it came back again to "Ellen West." The poem is composed of various forms: free verse, prosaic accounts of West's behavior from the psychiatrist himself, and even a gesture to the epistolary. "Ellen West" is creative non-fiction perhaps in its purest form.

When you begin teaching, you're always told not to bring in your favorite poems for your classes to discuss. If they don't like them, it'll ruin the work for you. That wasn't the case with me. My students were flummoxed: it's impossible to offer a thematic reading. They proved to me that Bidart has done the almost impossible: to show that the soul when composed through poetry can refuse to be reduced, simplified, obliterated, or even loved. Yet, it articulates *something* of importance. We can feel it. For better or worse, it escapes us. We have no words.

Charles A. Matz

A Poetry Before Oblivion: Five Rules

IN THE LATE 1960s, amid the anti-Vietnam War protests, Charles Matz came to the Southampton College English faculty from teaching at Notre Dame. He began performing his "shout" poetry—an antecedent of the larger genre called performance poetry—at Notre Dame, having been invited by his students to shake things up at a rock concert. He recalled that the rehearsal was raucous. "The clamber of noise extraordinary. I reasoned that I would have to create something that would match or exceed their volume level. The performance was before many rather staid nuns and priests. They were absolutely stunned. I had the students turn up the volume to blast people."

Despite his passion for performance, he continued to teach literature in Europe, England and the United States. In a diverse creative life, he also held the post of iconographer of nave clerestory windows, Washington National Cathedral.

1 Think that the poem is to be used. And that the poet is to be used. Used as though it were the last time, emergency, and the use was to consume them, use them up completely.

2 Conjure with the elements of the situation of use: setting, audience, time of day. Each use is a dramatic affair; prepare for it using theatrical methods . . .

3 Compose, if possible, for the precise usage. And repeat existing poems with extreme care & caution. In these emergency situations a used poem may not be adequate.

4 Keep in mind that the poem has to move out on three levels: first on the visual (and lesser) level, that is all the setting, lighting, room or open

space, the poet himself; then on the level of meaning (each word must be shaped to be understood, by rehearsal and intent at the moment of emergency use); and finally as music, being sounded with its rise and fall in dynamics, with the rhythmical beat clearly established and progressive, with tonality in proper pitch, in the voice.

5 Preserve an unbroken line in the performance. No faltering is possible. The whole shout will collapse if a moment's faltering and hesitancy is felt. Perfect self-assurance and control must be given to the hearers throughout, from opening words to climax and end. For safety, test the situation with the first words, or add preface words to prove out the ambient and the moment. Find the measure at once! The is an emergency. Remember: this is the last possible shout. Rouse yourself out of torpor and put everything into this last possible shout before oblivion.

David Lehman

Patricia Carlin

Ilya Kaminsky

Rusty Morrison

Denise Duhamel

Tony Trigilio

David Lehman

Introduction: The Birth of *The Best*

1.

Every September, a new edition of *The Best American Poetry* appears, quickening pulses, provoking arguments. From one year to the next, the editor's name on the cover is different, as is the cover art. The series editor is the one constant. It is the title I have held since the inaugural volume came out in 1988.

At bookstores and universities, or by digital means during and since the Covid pandemic, launch readings celebrate each new edition and let the public know which poems have gotten the nod from Sherman Alexie, Edward Hirsch, Natasha Trethewey, Dana Gioia, Major Jackson, Paisley Rekdal, Tracy K. Smith, and Matthew Zapruder, to name the successive guest editors since 2015. From 2003 through 2019, the New School in New York City, where I taught in the graduate writing program, sponsored an annual gathering of the year's contributors in a crowded lecture hall with five hundred seats. On one such occasion, more than forty of the seventy-five contributors took part, some flying in from as far away as California and Greece. In the green room, the pre-reading excitement was palpable.

As required reading in many college courses, *The Best American Poetry* is invariably on poetry best-seller lists—which may seem like an oxymoron, but isn't quite—reflecting data compiled from independent bookstores. Inclusion in the book is a feather in a poet's cap; not being chosen is, well, how many poets do you know who feel they have won the recognition they deserve? As series editor, I am sometimes confronted aggressively: how come my poem wasn't chosen for *Best American Poetry*? I resist saying "maybe you didn't write one of the year's best poems," and explain for what seems the hundredth time that even a capacious book of seventy-five poems cannot accommodate all the fine verse and prose poetry published in any twelve-month period in a nation as large, diverse, and multitudinous as the United States.

People may suppose that the anthology is part of a literary establishment, an institution of long standing. On the contrary, it existed only as an idea and not a fully-formed one, when it occurred to me as I drove from Ithaca to the nearby hamlet of Ludowville on the first Sunday in August 1987.

When Glen Hartley, my literary agent, submitted my proposal for *The Best American Poetry*, most publishing professionals thought that such a book as I had in mind would stand little chance of succeeding. Rejected by two publishers, both of them sympathetic but skeptical, *The Best American Poetry* became a reality only because an open-minded editor at a major trade house was able to suspend the industry-wide belief that books of poetry, good poetry, could not sell in sufficient quantity to make it worth the publisher's while. That editor was John Glusman, then with Scribner, which has been our publisher from the get-go. We have benefited greatly from the firm's editors, art directors, copy editors, proofreaders, and marketing personnel.

Every freelance writer has to be something of an entrepreneur. The entrepreneur in me is proud of having articulated a vison, refined the concept, persuaded a publisher to back it, and gone through all the stages, culminating not just in one book, but in a series of annual anthologies, year after year, one decade following another, across the century divide. Thirty-four years have gone by since *The Best American Poetry* made its debut. The 2022 volume reached me today (Sept 8, 2022), and I have three crowded bookshelves devoted to the series. Adding the two retrospective "Best of the Best" collections that appeared in 1998 and 2013, we now have published a total of thirty-six individual books.

My work as founder and series editor has enabled me to bear witness to what is happening in American poetry and to record my own observations in a sort of running commentary.

2.

At the same time that my BAP proposal was making the rounds in 1987, a renowned professor asked me whether I considered myself a critic or an editor first. A colleague of hers overheard and said, "He's a poet." Grateful for that recognition, I said that writing poetry was my reality, "an activity of the most august imagination," as Wallace Stevens defined "reality" in a late poem. Poetry is my base, but I never expected it to generate an income for me and I have always felt that writing prose and editing books and magazines were part of the deal.

I oppose the idea that one can be a specialist in one field only, or in one mode within that field. Why shouldn't we engage in as many interests as we had in college? I recall a year at Columbia during which I took courses in cinema, philosophy, modern British literature, Italian Renaissance painting, the English romantics, and the French symbolists. Why, then, need one limit oneself to one field of study or another? I have done a lot of different things: written poetry and nonfiction books, collaborated with artists and musicians, edited *The Oxford Book of American Poetry*, taught and lectured widely in the United States and abroad.

Nevertheless, I am glad the critic-or-editor question was raised if only because it prompted me to consider the relative importance to me of the various things I do. When put to it, I identify myself as a poet, an author, an editor, and a teacher in that order—by which I mean to imply that, for example, a poet wrote my books on Frank Sinatra, American popular song, murder mysteries and noir movies. As a self-employed writer, I see editing and literary journalism as ways of teaching by another name and reaching, at least potentially, more readers than can fit in a lecture room.

By temperament, I feel more comfortable praising than scolding, including rather than leaving out. The critic gets to elucidate poems, books, songs, films, and paintings; to air enthusiasms that may prove infectious. The editor of an anthology gets to work on behalf of others and for the sake of the art form. Both are well worth doing. The joy is grand when a piece of mine in the *Wall Street Journal* or *American Scholar* prompts readers to thank me for directing them to, say, George Herbert's "Love (III)" or Carol Reed's movie *Odd Man Out*. Equally grand is the joy of notifying a newcomer that her or his poem has been selected for *The Best American Poetry*—and hearing from them later that it changed their lives.

Other launch readings have taken place at Columbia, Seton Hall University, the Alliance Française and elsewhere in New York City through the auspices of the Academy of American Poets, New York University, the Huntington (Long Island) poetry festival organized by Faith Lieberman, and the Decatur Literary Festival in Atlanta.

Patricia Carlin

At Home

IN MY PARENTS' LIBRARY was a collection of Emily Dickinson poems. As a child of ten, I came across the book and kept it by my bed. Each night for a few weeks I memorized a poem selected at random. I chose these in no order, and not particularly for their meaning. I simply loved the sounds, the rhymes and the rhythms. Around then I decided I was going to be a poet.

By 12, I was a Dickinson acolyte. I felt I had a personal relationship with her. I was going to be a poet, I knew she'd been secretive about this ambition, and so was I. At about this same time, I remember being in our living room and hearing, from the radio in the next room, an English voice reciting the Death of Kings speech from Shakespeare's Richard II. I was completely mesmerized by the interwoven sounds and images. It was so extremely beautiful, tending to sheer music. Syntax, imagery, repetitions, vowel music, all the Shakespearean lyrical miracles were working, in a speech ending with Death himself making an entrance. Much later, as an adult, I realized that I'd been drawn to the Shakespeare speech for its mesmerizing lyric beauty, but also for its subject, death. My father was absent for much of my very early life, away in the navy. My grandfather had been a second father to me, and at five I had been alone with him when he died suddenly. As was typical of my family, this was never referred to then or afterwards. "Tell all the truth but tell it slant"—indirection is a hallmark of Dickinson's work, and indirection was my family's language and my language.

Tell all the Truth but tell it slant—
Success in Circuit lies
Too bright for our infirm Delight
The Truth's superb surprise
As Lightning to the Children eased

With explanation kind
The Truth must dazzle gradually
Or every man be blind—

The poem begins with "Truth" in the first line and introduces "lies" in the second line. "Lies" in this line means position, not untruth, but that other meaning of "lies" makes itself felt because of its proximity to the word "truth." The way a poem must tell the truth is compared to the way the fact of lightning must be presented to children—"eased / With explanation kind." The speaker is the kindly circuitous truthteller, and the readers are children who might be cruelly frightened if the truth about lightning were baldly presented. But the speaker is also one of the children. She and we, the readers, are enrolled together by the use of the word "our" in the phrase "our infirm Delight," both of us too weak to directly confront "the Truth's superb surprise."

Contradictory meanings co-exist in the poem, another form of slant truth-telling. "Truth must dazzle gradually" is a seeming impossibility, since to be dazzled means to be immediately struck. Further, "The Truth must dazzle gradually / Or every man be blind." People may be blinded by never seeing truth, or blinded by a too-abrupt, too direct encounter with that truth.

Truth, like a flash of lightning, is a "superb" source of surprise and delight and also potentially injurious, even lethal. Like lightning eased for children, poetry should be constructed to make something otherwise unbearable to the writer and the reader into something pleasing. The poem sets forth this project, and simultaneously illustrates its accomplishment in the poem. What I want to do in my work, and what many of the poems I love do, is to make dark or painful things pleasing—pleasing to me, and I hope to a reader—by drawing on multiple resources of language and technique.

Poetic influences are often absorbed unconsciously. Early on, from reading poets like Dickinson and Shakespeare, I internalized iambic rhythm. It took me years to root it out of my writing. That rhythm would creep in just when I wanted speech rhythms, or jagged or harsh sounds. I eventually learned how to make these competing elements jostle each other in expressive ways. An ongoing effort for me is to become aware of what I've internalized, so I can make conscious choices about what to use.

I consider myself fortunate that my earliest experience with poetry took place at home, not in school. There was no one to tell me what I should like, or what anything meant, or to interfere with my immediate physical pleasure in what I heard. I loved many poems before I had a clue as to what they meant. By the time I encountered poetry in college and then graduate school, I was fully inoculated against the kind of analysis that leads a reader far away from the actual experience of poems.

Ilya Kaminsky

Reading Dante in Ukraine

I HAVE A FRIEND WHO, before she ran from Kyiv as Russia bombarded the city in early 2022, spent weeks shivering in the bomb shelters as the city was shelled.

At first, she first recited poems by heart, and then she began to translate the poems she remembered.

That is how she got through the hours.

Who is to tell me after this that poetry doesn't matter?

·

Opening Dante's *Inferno* enrolls the reader in a millennium-long class in surviving hell with poetry, through music, imagery, and poetry's willingness to look without flinching at the details of both terror and wonder: in a strange way, this book is a call to courage.

But how?

The adventure begins in the spring of 1300 and lasts for seven days. What are these numbers, I wonder, to the reader who's about to enter the text like a pilgrim on their own journey? The poem is outside of history, like snow and rain and wind. The pilgrim Dante, poet and politician, barely thirty-five years old, and his guide, the shade of the dead poet Virgil, enter Hell at sunset, and spend the night and next day on foot, turning always to the left, as they go down the spiral. Reaching the center of the Earth, they cross beyond, to the other side of Satan, who's planted there: they are now on the opposite side of the hemisphere, gaining the time difference of twelve hours. They are headed for Purgatory, which they reach by morning. In the underworld, Dante meets his enemies and heroes—great thinkers, murderers, poets, politicians—but no one is too monumental. They are all trying to stay relevant to a living man, all too human, fragile, grotesque, not unlike ourselves, trying to say something that still matters.

Hell is other people, Sartre wrote, hundreds of years later. Turning the pages, we are aware that Alighieri's dead are shades, we see he is full of flesh and blood traveling among them, as if entering a busy subway station. What makes this journey so urgent is that while Dante is in hell he behaves like he is among us.

•

Hell is a city between Italy and Central Asia, a vast cavity in the form of an inverted cone, whose apex is at the center of the earth—Dante believed the earth to be perfectly spherical and about twenty thousand miles in circumference.

I can't help but wonder about a reader opening the book for the first time, perhaps in Italy, or perhaps in wartime Ukraine, several miles from here, perhaps you yourself, among flames and faces of people who were once alive, people who shout at you now, though they have no mouths, people you hate and love.

Night emerges into their faces.

Turn left, and watch the roads. The clang of each voice is like a lamp among stones.

Here we are, reading this version of an old poem, reading it in American English, while the majority of people in our country are numb to all sorts of crises of our own.

Here we are in 2022, in *Purgatorio*, which was once a *Paradiso* of a planet we harmed, and which through our species' actions, is about to turn into a hell.

What is the role of language in this?

The normative language of any time period—but especially the normative language of a twenty-first-century capitalist empire such as ours (e.g., words like "collateral damage" instead of an evocative image of a child shot dead by a soldier in the street) is specifically intended to numb us.

Dante understands this: in his own time of political upheaval, he fills the pages with images, metaphors, unpredictable rhythms. He fills proverbial hell with conflicts of his then present moment. For example, Filippo Argenti opposed Dante's return from exile and stole the poet's possessions for himself. So, Dante uses his language as a weapon: he puts Argenti in the fifth circle of Hell. Poetry, by definition, opposes the normative, the dull. The poem wakes us up; it must actively cast a spell on the reader *now*. Regardless of its subject. *That freshness of speech ravishes the human in us.*

•

Somewhere in Ukraine right now, my friend who publishes books orders printers in the bombed-out city of Kharkiv to produce thousands of copies of the *Inferno*. The trucks deliver weapons into Kharkiv. And, going back, empty, they decide to pick up thousands of copies of Dante's *Inferno*.

This is an image of war that happens as I write it: cars are bringing weapons into the besieged city that's bombed daily, and they leave full of books.

·

For me, as one reader, this is what poetry is: not a kind of public posturing, but a private language of music and vivid imagery that is strange and compelling enough that it can speak privately and evocatively to thousands of people at the same time.

That is why it just doesn't die, poetry—despite so many death notices. It is always there, waking us up when we get numb, poking us in the eye.

·

Meanwhile, here in the United States, my favorite English translator of this text is Henry Wadsworth Longfellow, who understood all too well this ability to shelter oneself with poetry when a crisis comes. The story of Longfellow's own decision to translate Dante's great poem of turmoil is compelling, and instructive for us today—he did so as a way of coping with his grief after the traumatic loss of his beloved young wife, who died when her dress caught on fire.

Just as Virgil, beloved poet, teacher and guide (who lived almost as many years before Dante as Dante himself lived before Longfellow) helps our pilgrim to cope, the translator turns toward the *Inferno* in American English, to confront his own monsters, now in translation, learning how to continue, one word at a time, on his sometimes terrible path of grief.

·

Over seven centuries after Dante's birth, when a Ukrainian city is bombed, a woman hiding in the subway station recites the lines of poetry to herself and others around her. A line of poetry is a kind of invisible shield, a moment of charged silence, a bit of awe, that we carry from one human body to another, that we transport by means of language. That memorable speech, however horrifying its subject matter might be, offers us a balm, offers us a way to go on.

And so today, in 2022, in our own time of crisis, we can hear the echo of Dante in his crisis of exile, as we might hear another exile, Bertolt Brecht, whispering in the middle of World War Two:

In the dark times
Will there also be singing?
Yes, there will also be singing.
About the dark times.

Poetry doesn't matter, contemporary American culture seems to insist. But this book begs to differ. Dante and his contemporaries have long been laid in the holes in the earth, drowned in rivers, burnt inside their homes during endless wars.

Their bodies have been deposited into the planet.

But this book continues its journey above it. It meets us. The pilgrim keeps walking on.

Dante has no need to defend his art. *Poetry matters*: he sees it as a primal ancient force and art form, one that's been here long before our individual lifetimes and will stay long after (Virgil, who lived centuries before him, guides him into the present). What we need, Dante's journey shows us, is to defend ourselves *with* it: a tune to walk to, even in the underworld, as long as one still walks.

I open the book and read poems aloud while somewhere the car full of guns is driving at full speed into the city of Kharkiv, and in a few hours, when it is leaving the city on fire, the car, driving over sidewalks, without stopping at streetlights, hurrying to get out, is filled with books.

Rusty Morrison

Writing into risk

What it feels like to pay attention to the limitations I live with in my daily life

BEFORE I BEGAN WRITING my most recently published book, *RISK*, I was struggling with limitations, which I felt were mostly caused by forces beyond my control: bouts of difficult illnesses and injuries, challenges in my work, and my husband's death from cancer. And after his death, I was alone with the precarious, risky state of our finances.

In retrospect, I see that I felt victimized by my life, and how that feeling pervaded my experience, making it difficult to trust what the future might hold.

Writing has always been a solace for me, and, more than a solace, a way to see with compassion what is happening in my life. It has always been through writing that I've discovered a wider awareness, and found the steps I might take to act upon what that awareness offered me.

Though I wasn't clear about how victimized I felt, I did know that I needed help. I returned to a regular, daily, writing practice, early in the morning. In this work, I found more ease, more willingness to face the day's challenges. This alone was of great value, but there was more.

I began to consider how I might use a form to enliven my work. I found that writing in a *limiting form* could give me a direct experience of what it feels like *to live in the limitations*. As I continued this work, I began to ask myself which were unavoidable, and which were subtly self-inflicted by negative feelings that I'd let impact me. By using a constraining form, I would not just write *about limitation*, I'd live inside limitation in the work and then see how I handled it. I would experience limitation as event, not aftermath.

Most of the poems in *RISK* have 14 syllables in each line with a caesura between the first seven syllables and the last seven syllables. I did not break a word at the end of each seven syllables, so I had to use constant revision. I wanted this approach to let me experience formally how challenging it is to keep my life in flow, and how surprising it can be to try something unexpected and have it bring meaningful balance into my life.

Besides these poems, there are also poems scattered through the manuscript that are titled "Narrow Negotiations." In these, the form is this: each has exactly seven couplets (14 lines per poem). Each line in the poem has seven syllables (as does the title "Narrow Negotiations").

Ann Lauterbach points out that the "convergence of subject matter with form releases content." I found that the forms I created caused a contentiousness in my use of syntax that forced me to diverge from my more expected trajectories of thought, and so the forms exposed a content with more contextual resources than I'd previously had access to.

But contrived structures can obscure as much as they reveal; my obsessions are powerful. I had to let the poems continue to ask me if I was writing in support of my intuitions about freedom or if I was sometimes avoiding them. Once I saw, in the writing, how easily I could delude myself, I started to see it in my life.

Hélène Cixous tells us that "the border makes up the homeland, it prohibits and gives passage in the same stroke." My work is to see where the borders, which I use to contain my understandings, are actually useful, and where they are borders that I must open and pass beyond, frightening as that might be.

One more thing comes to mind to say—the ways I work with Omnidawn poets, and poets to whom I give consultations, is the same way that I work with myself. With them, I believe strongly in creating a collaborative process that remains dynamic as we work from page to page, or image to image in a poem. With myself, I believe I must listen collaboratively to all the selves I am and let them all impact the poem.

I think of this work as comparable to sitting at a Ouija board. But rather than spirits talking to me, or me talking to another poet, it's the poem's true heart speaking into our hands. The board is the poem, intuitions combine (my many intuitions when I'm making my own poems or the other poet's intuitions along with mine, when I'm working with another poet). In that combination it's possible to hear how the poem wants to move the "planchette or movable indicator."

This process is a form of spiritual practice to me. I am grateful for the ways it sustains me.

Denise Duhamel

In Praise of Colette Inez's "Pay Yourself First"

IN 1990 I HAD THE PLEASURE of reading with Colette Inez in a library in Tarrytown, NY. We bonded immediately—we were both wearing all black. We both had (dyed) red hair. We were both Geminis with June birthdays. We were both of French heritage. Colette had a French mother and French-American father who was really a Father (a priest!) which deserves its own essay, of course, and of which she wrote brilliant poems and a heart wrenching memoir *The Secret of M. Dulong*.

Colette Inez (1931-2018) was like a poetry fairy godmother to me. I'd finished grad school by the time we met. My poetry professors, quite rightly, were busy helping their new students. Colette's advice was wacky and fun. She said it was important to wear black—or solid colors—for readings so that the audience would be focused on the poet's face rather than any patterned blouse or dress. She also advised big earrings and bright lipstick as other ways to draw attention to the poet's head and mouth. Colette had an elegant, easy-going style, quick to smile and laugh. But the best advice of all she bestowed (her metaphorical wand touching the top of my head) was this—*always pay yourself first.* I was an adjunct those days, teaching six classes a semester at three different universities, my arduous commute taking me from Manhattan to Long Island and Queens. I didn't at first understand what she meant by "pay."

Colette asked when I did my best writing and I said, *Whenever I can. Whenever I am done grading and preparing my next classes.* She explained that wouldn't sustain me over the long haul and repeated her question. I told her I wrote best in the morning, but often, when I woke up, anxiety took over in terms of all I had to do for that particular day. She explained that I had to first feed myself with poetry—that's what she meant by *pay yourself first*—allow myself an hour of writing per day first thing in the morning if I could. If nothing came to the page, I was allowed to fill that time with reading poetry. She instructed me to stroll right by my piles of ungraded papers and unpaid bills, ignore them completely. Her voice was so confident that I did what she said, setting a timer and writing an hour each morning. Sometimes I wrote nothing much or *I guess I don't have anything to say today*, but every few days I had a breakthrough.

Colette and I kept in touch through letters for the remainder of her life. We sent each other poems and postcards. For more than thirty years I have heeded her counsel. It has made me, certainly, a better and more disciplined writer. It has also, I believe, made me a better professor. No longer do I feel resentful of grading. I am lucky—I teach poetry now rather than comp classes and grading is not so much grading as engaging with student poems.

I have adapted Colette's advice as technology marched on. Now, in addition to ignoring bills and correspondence, I also try to avoid email for my first hour of the day and spend that time writing and reading. I keep the volume of my cellphone off until I am ready to deal with any calls or texts. And when I do finally check my email, I open the Poem-a-Day email before any work emails. And only after all that do I check the news. It's a small practice but one that has kept me sane and writing poetry. When Colette and I met, the words "selfcare" or "me time" weren't part of the vernacular yet, and I hesitate to use them now. But there was something profound about Colette's writing advice—which had nothing to do with craft but everything to do with process—that has been invaluable to me.

More than once I have passed on this same advice to younger poets who now must struggle with all the issues I did as a young person as well as keeping up with social media. I am not on any platforms myself, yet I know how important this way of communicating is to many. Trying to channel Colette, I suggest poets keep that hour to themselves, whenever they write best. One former student recently told me it was not until we spoke about this that she even realized she could turn off her notifications. I'd tapped my metaphorical wand on her head, and she passed on Colette's advice via me through her own wand, to her poet friends on Facebook. Then she put her phone in a drawer and began to write in her notebook.

Tony Trigilio

The Importance of Being Obstinate

IT WAS THE YEAR 2008, and I'd just finished reading from my first book of poems, *The Lama's English Lessons,* at Schlafly Bottleworks in St. Louis. I stood with my back pressed against the bar as the next reader took the stage. A member of the audience, a young man who looked to be in his early twenties, walked over.

He said he enjoyed my poems. Then he asked, "What advice do you have for a writer who's just starting out?"

I'd been teaching undergraduate and graduate student poets at Columbia College Chicago for nearly ten years already. I was comfortable in my professorial identity. Dispensing writing advice is an integral part of the job. But right now, as I leaned against a bar in St. Louis, I found myself trying to offer guidance to a younger writer outside the four walls of the classroom, beyond the comfortable boundaries of the fifteen-week semester and the three-hour class session, far removed from curriculum plans and assigned texts. I feared that if I said the wrong thing, I might derail his fledgling writing career. This feeling that I had the power to disrupt another writer's career trajectory was a result of bravado on my part; at the time, I worried that my first book of poems might either be panned or, worse, ignored. Deep down, I wasn't confident I could offer any meaningful reply to his question.

I had no more than a few minutes to respond before the next reader began. She was situating herself at the microphone and I didn't want to be rude and hold a conversation with someone else while she was reading.

"Be stubborn," I blurted out. The words came to me spontaneously. I'd never before encouraged a student to consider obstinacy as a poetics.

My father was the most obstinate man I'd ever met. I loved him immensely, yet his stubbornness strained his relationship with my mother and, at times, with my siblings and me. Even so, I unconsciously absorbed his obstinance into my own personality, which, no surprise, sometimes made it difficult for me to sustain friendships and relationships. I had driven alone to St. Louis for the reading. I didn't realize it yet, but my first marriage was on the verge of ending, and my stubborn personality played no small role in the breakup.

Still, I repeated, "You really just have to be stubborn."

He looked at me strangely, as if disappointed that I hadn't talked about, for instance, my writing process or my strategy for submitting work to journals and presses. I realized I should say more, and that I had to do it quickly so that I could hear the next reader.

"You need to have a persistent belief in the power of your imagination, a faith in your creative process that runs so deep that you're too stubborn to give up."

"That's all? You have to believe you're a good writer. That's it."

I nodded.

"But everyone feels this way."

"You don't want to believe in your work when it's no good," I added, leaning forward, lowering my voice as the writer on stage thanked the reading series curators and the brewery. I could feel a soliloquy coming on. A friend of mine once said the reason Nathaniel Hawthorne is one of my favorite writers is that, like him, I talk in paragraphs.

I tried to be brief so that we could both hear the next reader.

"You want to believe in yourself so much that when obstacles get in the way, like rejections from editors, you can stubbornly persist anyway. You don't want to be so obstinate that you ignore editors when they say a piece of writing isn't ready to be published. By 'stubborn,' I mean that you believe in yourself so much that when you get rejection after rejection after rejection, which happens to almost every writer, you don't lose your commitment to making your writing better."

He took a step backward. He was either considering the merits of what I was saying, or he had decided to just put some distance between us and end the conversation. "Stubbornness" was not what I'd expected to say, nor, it seemed, was it within the realm of writerly advice he'd expected to hear.

"It's hard enough being an artist in a utilitarian culture that doesn't really value what we make or do," I added. "You don't want to make things worse by allowing the outside world to destroy your belief that your own imaginative labor can make you a better writer."

Another awkward pause. Then he asked me to sign his copy of the book.

I kept thinking about this conversation during the five-hour drive back to Chicago the next day. I couldn't figure out why I reached for "stubbornness" in response to this audience member who clearly had put forth the kind of fundamental question that is a typical feature of question-and-answer sessions with audiences at the end of readings.

In such situations, you're usually asked about how to submit individual poems or essays to literary journals, how to put together a full manuscript and where to send manuscripts, how to find the discipline required to complete a full-length book, and so on—all manner of pragmatic, nuts-and-bolts questions that emerging writers, naturally, want answered. Looking back now, one of the reasons I went straight for the more esoteric answer was, simply, that I'm not convinced that good writing advice can emerge from the kind of one-size-fits-all environment of the usual post-reading question-and-answer session.

I was still relatively new to the publishing world, and my primary concern that night in St. Louis was for the poems from my new book to connect with an audience. But even then, I was suspicious of the expectation I'd seen so often from my fellow audience members at readings that if you asked the right question, in just the right way, the writer would deliver a bullet-point list of how-to advice that, like a magic spell, would launch your writing career. In hindsight, I don't think the person who asked me "What advice do you have for a writer who's just starting out?" was looking for an easy fix. But I felt this way back then—and, worse, I didn't believe I had quite enough experience yet to give him a satisfying answer.

Instead of taking a pragmatic approach to his query, I responded with something orphic, as if I were pointing to the word "stubborn" in the middle of a poem and asking him to hold the word up to the light and turn it in multiple angles of vision to see just how many refracted meanings he could come up with. I wondered if his hesitance, especially his long pause before asking me to sign the book, was an indication that I had disappointed him. I truly wanted to answer his question, but my altruistic intent was far removed from what became its confusing impact. At the same time, I felt—and still do—that I gave him a valuable answer.

I still believed in my response, in the value of writerly stubbornness, but as I drove home, I tried to figure out why stubbornness had been so squarely on my mind the previous evening after the reading.

I remembered something one of my percussion teachers, Dave Robinson, said to me back in my early twenties. Dave was the drummer for The Numbers Band, an avant-blues group with an enormous Midwest following. They were the house band at JBs, in Kent, Ohio, where I was an undergraduate student at Kent State University. Dave and I were discussing a particularly complicated, alternating-accent triplet beat that had taken weeks for me to master. For this lesson, I proudly showed off a modified version of the beat—a simpler, stripped-down variation that fit a new song that my band, Incline, was working on. I played my version for him then scanned his face for the wry, crooked smile that always told me I had impressed my teacher.

"What you played works fine," he said eventually. "It's steady and it has a dynamic pattern. Good variation. But it doesn't sing like the original version we've been working on."

I straightened myself in the chair. I'd expected unconditional approval and was surprised that I felt the need to defend myself.

"I like how my version fits the song we're writing. It comes off a little less pretentious than the original beat you played for me. Like you always say, I don't want to just show off my chops on stage."

At that time in my life, what held me back the most as a musician was that I absolutely wanted nothing more than to demonstrate virtuosity on stage, even if this came at the expense of the songs themselves. Dave, as my drum teacher, knew this better than anyone.

"But when you really think about it, nothing's more pretentious than assuming other people want to come to a club and pay a cover charge to hear you play music," he said. "We all need to feel 'pretentious' just to get on stage at all. Just to assume an audience cares enough to want to see you play. Even when you're having a bad day, you have to go into a show with the total expectation that you're talented enough for people to think they're going to have a good time watching you perform."

He was right, of course. As I recalled Dave's remarks on my drive home from St. Louis, I realized the extent to which I'd absorbed his peculiar—but useful—redefinition of "pretentious." We're often taught that pretension is a character flaw, the result of an overweening, and unearned, belief in one's talent and importance. But Dave helped me see a flip side to pretension. In his reformulation, the word felt more like an honorable form of audacity. How audacious to think that an audience wanted to go to a club and pay to see my band perform songs we'd written and rehearsed in our moldy basement studio. But without such audacity, it would be too easy to surrender to the fear that I might fail, that an audience would leave one of our shows regretting they'd come in the first place. Wasn't stubbornness, then, just a variation of the kind of pretension and audacity that allows you to believe you have something to say—and believe other people want to hear it?

Stubbornness is a complicated personality trait, especially for someone like myself who grew up watching my father's stubbornness alienate his family. Stubbornness can quell the fear that we have nothing to say, but it also can be a manifestation of insecurity. When I doubt myself, I tend to talk over, or ignore, the opposing viewpoints of others. Digging in my heels is often a manifestation of uncertainty, of wanting to (stubbornly) control a situation that could become chaotic. As vital as it is to believe in yourself, an inflated self-regard can be nothing but narcissism.

But even though pretension and stubbornness can be nothing but bluster, they also can provide the extra spark of confidence to propel you to make art. If not for a stubborn belief in the importance of your work, you might never leave that moldy basement studio and perform. Art is, at its core, a mode of communication with others, and sometimes it's only stubbornness and pretension that allow us to share our work with an audience—that prevent us from talking only to ourselves.

Mary Mackey

Sandy McIntosh

Denise Low

Jim Natal

Elaine Equi

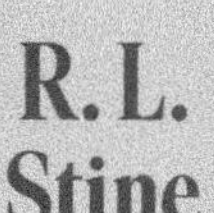

R. L. Stine

Phillip Lopate

Mary Mackey

The Quest for Inspiration

> Plants and animals pass into one another, a perpetual metempsychosis of protective coloration. Forms, colors, and patterns converge generating an organic colloid; foreground and background blend by mutual accommodation.
>
> A stick is floating down the river, drifting towards the pool below the bridge. As it passes the edge of the gravel triangle (just below the mouth of the creek), it suddenly turns, slides up the bank, and coils itself around a warm rock. As it dries in the sun, the bark begins to turn to scales.
>
> from *Immersion*
> Mary Mackey, Shameless Hussy Press, 1972

IT'S THE FALL OF 1969, and I am sitting in the University of Chicago Main Library at a small oak table by a large, dirty window that is covered by a hefty iron screen. Unlike the window screens in private homes, this one is installed on the inside as if it had been designed to prevent people from escaping. The tabletop is scarred with the marks of generations of library users who have marred its surface with scratches, rings from illicit cups of coffee, and, in one notable instance, small parallel gouges that appear to be the work of either a frustrated, long-toothed graduate student or a rogue beaver.

To my left sits a large black plastic ashtray, because incredible as it may seem, in 1969 smoking is still permitted in this building, which holds well over ten million inflammable books and sixty-five thousand linear feet of irreplaceable archives and manuscripts. Directly in front of me sit a blank notebook and three refillable fountain pens. To my right is a bank of tall metal bookcases filled with books, which it appears no one ever reads.

During the three days I have been coming here to stare at the notebook and not so much as pick up one of the pens, I have not seen another human being wandering through this part of the stacks, and that's fine by me. In fact, I planned it this way. This is the Scandinavian Statistics Section, perhaps the most unused and least frequented part of the Library, a place where presumably people who can read Swedish only come if they want to find out how many bear fur cloaks, if any, were exported on a yearly basis from the eleventh-century proto-Swedish kingdom of *Sverige*.

The silence is so complete, I can hear the blood pumping through my ears. If there is a quieter place on earth, I have yet to find it.

I look again at the window screen, the tabletop, the ashtray, the pens, the battered books leaning against one another like drunks staggering home after a memorable Saturday night. I note all these details again and again, because I am procrastinating. I am about to do something momentous, and I don't have the slightest idea how to go about it: I'm about to write my first novel. And not just any novel.

It's a crazy idea, really: to write a novel that will create in the reader a sense of what it is like to be part of the jungle, to be as inseparable from it as the trees. Is it possible to use words to plunge people into a superorganism of almost over a billion parts that is a whole in itself and in many ways as beyond words as the landscape of dreams is beyond description? Is it possible to blend the vocabularies of science and literature, to use the vocabularies of biologists, zoologists, physicists, geneticists, novelists, and poets and merge them into a single, coherent whole, which, like the jungle is more than the sum of its parts? Is it possible to create a plot and characters that will encompass these ambitions—for all novels must have plots and characters?

I don't know, but I have just finished my doctoral dissertation, and I figure that if I can write a 350-page non-fiction scholarly thesis, I must have a novel in me, so I've decided to give it a try. The timing is right. The vice of focused rationality that has sustained me during my years in graduate school has begun to loosen its grip, and a host of ideas and images has flooded my mind. For the first time since I graduated from college, I have begun to remember my dreams.

I open the notebook and pick up one of the pens. I have no idea how or where to start, so I decide to begin with a description of the ashtray that sits at my left elbow. I will look at this ashtray intently. I will see it as if I had never seen it before, I will view it as an alien artifact created for some unknown purpose. I will describe it so that it cannot be confused with any other ashtray ever created. I will search out, find, and resurrect the way I saw the world as a very young child—a world in which categories did not yet exist, in which there was no context, no expectation, no reason not to look at the unimportant details of things as well as the important ones.

Beginning a novel about the jungle with a description of an ashtray may seem like an odd choice, but recently I have become increasingly aware of a strange phenomenon: if you look at any object long enough and intently enough, it becomes incomprehensible. Put another way, it no longer has a stable appearance, but will shift back and forth taking on different forms and changing size and shape as you stare at it.

I first came across this odd characteristic of the physical world as a sophomore at Harvard in an undergraduate Social Sciences course taught by Jerome Bruner, a psychologist renowned for his research relating to cognitive psychology and educational psychology. During the semester, Professor Bruner occasionally invited the class to participate in his research in harmless and fascinating ways that never caused anyone the slightest distress. This was in sharp contrast to the recent experiments with LSD that former Harvard Professor Timothy Leary had allowed his students to participate in—the ones that had gotten Leary fired from Harvard the spring of my freshman year.

On this particular morning, Professor Bruner had brought a series of slides to class which he projected onto a large screen. The slides were all of inanimate objects. When each slide first appeared, it was so out of focus that all we could see was a mass of undifferentiated colors. Professor Bruner explained that he would slowly bring each slide into focus and that we were to raise our hands when we could identify the object.

I only remember one slide. As it gradually came into focus, I initially saw the indistinct outline of a circle. With more clarity, I became convinced that I was looking at a beautiful aerial photograph of a great circular stadium constructed of warm brown tiles. It looked huge—perhaps it seated thousands.

Professor Bruner continued to make the image sharper. All around me hands were going up, but mine remained in my lap. A stadium. Yes, a stadium. But . . . I couldn't put my finger on the little thread of doubt that lingered in my mind. But . . . something.

At last the image lay before me in perfect clarity. I stared at the stadium, admired its grandeur, put up my hand, and Professor Bruner asked me what I saw.

"A stadium," I said. "A huge stadium seen from the air." There was laughter.

"It's a manhole cover," Professor Bruner said. The moment he uttered those words, the stadium shrunk, and I realized with a shock that what I had assumed was a huge object was in fact a fairly small one, and that for a good two minutes, I had been staring at a perfectly clear photograph of an ordinary, slightly-rusted manhole cover without being able to identify it. The problem was: I had made up my mind early on that I was looking at a stadium, and once that happened, I had become trapped in the wrong category; whereas if I had initially seen the manhole cover in focus, I never would have gotten the scale of it so wrong. All of which was exactly the point of Professor Bruner's experiment.

I turn my attention to the ashtray and stare at it just as I stared at that slide of the manhole cover: intensely, unwaveringly only this time instead of trying to identify it, I try not to identify it. Sure enough, within a few seconds, the ashtray begins to shift and change and become both meaningless the way the word "the" becomes meaningless if you say it a hundred times and filled with possibilities the way all objects become filled with possibilities before you file them in the right pigeonhole.

> **A black hole. A void. A revolving wheel. A floating disc. An inkblot on the flat, two-dimensional surface of the tabletop without borders or depth . . .**

I believe I am trying to begin writing a novel by freeing up my imagination from received categories, and indeed, that is what I am doing. But I am also doing something else, something that will be so central to the way I write poems that it will change the whole way I go about creating them. I am teaching myself the art of entering a state of hyper-objectivity, a state of extreme focus. I am teaching myself to stare fixedly at the world and expect nothing but what comes from that staring. At the same time, I am re-living and re-learning the essence of metaphor that I experienced at the age of eleven when I sat at a wooden desk looking out a window at falling leaves and saw that they contained geometric patterns within their irregular shapes.

In the years since I wrote my first poem, I have become convinced that the element of comparison in metaphor is not an accident but is innate in all things. It is the quality of objects being able to look like other objects if you concentrate on them intently enough. So I sit staring at an ashtray, because I believe this kind of hyper-focus is one of the keys to the creation of rich, layered, complex poetry, and also, I hope, turn out to be the key to a rich, layered, complex novel.

> Cool smooth blank a hole a dark spot shadow of a leaf trembling on one edge or do the edges go beyond out beyond like auras unidimensional so where it ends and the tabletop begins there is no way to tell and do you have to describe everything to describe one thing is there is no separation . . . and . . .

For the better part of twenty minutes, I go on describing the ashtray in the most minute detail possible, trying to see it without expectations of any kind, and then, all at once, the first lines of my novel appear beneath my hand like a shoal of whales breaching out of the ocean. I write:

> Eduardo is drowning.
>
> Rocking from side to side, he moves like a swimmer—head up, eyes open, fingers pressed tightly together. A neurotoxin is paralyzing his central nervous system, depressing respiration, sending his body into a series of involuntary convulsions.
>
> (Closing my eyes, I stop the motion, reverse the sequence.)

I stop and re-read what I have written. What do I have here? A boy or perhaps a man christened with the Spanish version of my father's middle name. An *Eduardo*, dying of snakebite in a jungle pool for reasons unknown. A narrator of unrevealed gender who I suspect is female, one who moves between first and third person, between present time and memory, with no apparent appreciation that there is a difference between the two. A kind of baptism, a total bodily immersion that may bring some kind of revelation, although I can't imagine what that revelation will be.

> Eduardo. The jungle. Immersion.

It's a beginning.

This is enough for one day. I close the notebook, pack up my pens, pick up my bookbag, and leave the Scandinavian Statistics Section to the great silence of its unread books.

I will come back repeatedly, day after day, to write more on *Immersion*, this novel which I will never outline but simply watch unfold out of my imagination like the blooming of a great tropical flower.

Slowly, the plot will appear, at first in pieces, then as a whole. The narrator is a young woman named Kirsten. Isolated in a remote field station in a tropical rainforest, she wages a desperate struggle for intellectual, spiritual, personal, and sexual liberation from her lover who views her as a piece of property and the creatures of the rainforest as specimens to be killed and catalogued. The result of this tangle of jealousy, betrayal, and relentless tropical heat leads to murder but of an unexpected victim. And behind and within the plot and characters lies the jungle, that great living creature of a billion parts that Kirsten merges with, loses herself in. Becomes.

I write *Immersion* at a time when I have unbecome a poet, a time when I believe I can no longer write poetry. I write this novel while simultaneously trying unsuccessfully to recapture something important that I have lost. From 1969 to 1970, I put hundreds of would-be poetic lines down on paper, but they are lifeless, and none of them fall together to form so much as a haiku. I try to season my attempts with metaphors and unusual images, but the result is flat, contrived, labored, and mechanical. While *Immersion* flows smoothly, while I find writing it almost effortless, the poems I produce during this period are so bad they are embarrassing.

At one point, I even enter a contest I come across while, for some inexplicable reason, reading *Cat Magazine*. First prize for the best cat poem is twenty dollars. I can definitely use the twenty dollars, which is about what my groceries cost every month, but no matter how hard I try, I can no more write a poem about cats than I can write a poem about deep-well oil drilling. My ability to write poetry seems to have skipped town, and I have no reason to believe it will ever return.

By the summer of 1970, when I head to California to look for a teaching job, I have finished *Immersion*. It is not a long novel: only 126 pages, but in it I've done what I wanted to do. When I get to Berkeley, I make friends with Pat and Fred Cody, owners of Cody's Books, which at the time is one of America's great bookstores. I give them the manuscript of *Immersion*. They read it and are so impressed that, to my surprise and delight, Fred offers to become my agent—something I don't believe he has ever done before.

He is on a first name basis with most of the editors at the major publishing houses in New York, and he promptly submits *Immersion* to them with glowing letters of recommendation which say, among other things, that it is the most amazing, brilliantly written novel he has ever read. This is wonderfully encouraging, but it goes nowhere.

The editors send back rejection letters all of which more or less say the same thing: "Mary Mackey is an extraordinarily talented writer. This is indeed a brilliant novel. We have never seen anything like it. We want to publish it, but we can't see anyway to market it. It's too unusual. It's simultaneously cinematic, poetic, and hallucinatory. There's probably not a bookstore in the world that would know which shelf to put it on."

I read and re-read the letters of rejection and learn two things. First: if you want to get a novel published, you have to write one that will sell. Second: novels that sell are novels that are like other novels that have sold. Trying to re-invent the novel only leads to sitting around reading letters of rejection.

And I learn a third thing: In all those years when I thought I had unbecome a poet, in those years when I thought I couldn't write poetry, I had unconsciously been writing it, day after day, hour after hour.

Immersion, with all its passion, character revelation, struggle, quest for identity, and murder-mystery plot is definitely a novel.

But it is also a 126-page poem.

> A mist net is strung along the opposite side of the river. Hundreds of fine black threads (invisible against the background vegetation) are suspended between the guaybo trees. Intersecting at right angles, two sets of parallel lines cross to form a huge rectangle, bloated into three dimensions at the center, stretched out along the edges.
>
> Suddenly a hummingbird appears, flying straight toward the upper right-hand corner of the net. As it strikes the webbing, it's flight continues for a moment without interruption. The bird moves forward rapidly as if unaware of the surrounding threads. Then, abruptly, the net closes in . . .

from *Immersion*
Mary Mackey Shameless Hussy Press

Sandy McIntosh

Coaxing the Hangman

DAVID IGNATOW HAD BEEN at his kitchen table reading an article in *The New York Times.* "Did you ever hear of 'Drop Weight'?" he asked, pointing to the newspaper. "Drop Weight is how they measure the strength of a rope needed to hang a man. If the man is too heavy, a thin rope will unravel. And, if he's fat, and they measured wrong, the whole gallows will split apart, and the guy will drop down and still be alive. So, maybe a way to think of a good poem is like a man who's hanged: The rope must be just right, and the apparatus strong enough, so the body drops, and the neck is snapped. One clean motion."

We'd both been invited to read our poems at the home of H. R. Hays. "So, don't read that Vietnam poem," Ignatow continued, "unless you cut out all that adolescent bullshit about getting drafted and write something concise. Make your poem clean and make it snap!"

H. R. Hays was a poet and the early translator of Bertolt Brecht, and Spanish-American poets much praised by Robert Bly and others. Invited also were his neighbors, members of the Hamptons, Long Island poetry community, including Harvey Shapiro, editor of *The New York Times Book Review,* Allan Planz, poetry editor of *The Nation* and others. Ignatow warned: "You don't want them thinking less of you, spoiling your reputation before you have one. Read the poem Hays asked for, the one about Eisenhower's funeral."

But, at Hays' party, after I'd read the Eisenhower poem, the writers applauded and asked me to read an encore. I flipped through my notebook in a panic looking for something fit to read. Under the harsh light of the audience's attention, the horrible realization settled on me that all the notebook poems I was so proud of were terrible! I'd been carrying around an impressive, overstuffed valise, showing off, but there was little good in it. All were truly bad except that poem about Vietnam Ignatow had criticized. I was certain if I found it, I'd prove Ignatow wrong.

I couldn't find it. I flipped through the pages sensing the audience's disquiet. At last, in a bid to keep their attention I recited it from memory.

The reaction was gratifying laughter and applause. Allan Planz came up to me and asked if he could publish the poem in *The Nation*. My first thought was that I had been right and Ignatow wrong: it was a great poem.

Later, in the car driving home, I recalled my triumph. I heard the applause, but as I mentally played back my recitation, I noticed that the poem was quite short—much shorter than the one I'd shown to Ignatow, which must have been about seventy or eighty lines. What had happened? I had titled it: "America Before the Revolution" and dedicated it to the "Bomb-Them-Back-to-the-Stone Age" general Curtis LeMay.

Driving along, I recited the poem as I remembered reciting it:

Sir:
How I enjoyed
Your words last night
About this being God's war. I was so excited
That I didn't notice eating my mother
Who had fallen into her own apple pie.

What I recited had been only six lines long. What happened to the other seventy?

At home, I found the original version and read it through. Ignatow had been correct. Except for those first six lines, everything else was self-indulgent bullshit. It was as if, having written those lines and realizing that I had something there, I decided to take the opportunity to cash in on the listener's attention by delivering a sermon.

Idiotic as my assumption had been, I realized that there was something inside me that had known the score all along. A silent editor who, if I listened, would guide me in the right direction. Propelled by panic, I had recited only the necessary lines that, as Ignatow pointed out, would open the trapdoor to let the body fall and the neck snap. One clean motion. The invisible hangman: the better maker.

Denise Low

Gary Snyder and a Lesson in Consistency

Looking for Your Blue Spot

We always heard Asian babies have blue spots,
blue splotches of pigment on their bottoms
so at your first bath we turned you over.
There glowed a blue quarter
at the base of your spine like a scar
where someone yanked off your tail
and higher up your back
floated indigo Madagascar. . . .

(adapted from *Dragon Kite*, BkMk Press)

I SHOWED GARY SNYDER an early draft of this poem, and I remember learning how the word "yanked" was out of place in this sweet portrait of my toddler son. I was proud of the "Madagascar" image, the chewy word "splotches," and the quarter. I thought I had created a good poem. Gary cocked his head sideways and gently said . . .

First, some background. In the late 1970s in Lawrence, Kansas, my hometown, Gary Snyder was an avatar, in the original sense of that word. He came to the University of Kansas art museum several times to participate in talks related to the museum's fine Japanese print collection. He had just won the Pulitzer Prize in poetry a few years before. We writers and Asian art aficionados of Lawrence also understood he was one of the first advocates for Zen Buddhism in the United States. As a poet, a Zen practitioner, and a Beat writer, he was a living legend.

We were in awe of the great man, in a very un-Zenlike manner. Here is a measure of his impact, no exaggeration: So many started having visitation dreams about Snyder that later they were collected into a journal publication.

During one of Gary's visits, the university English department engaged him to work with graduate students, my status at the time. Robin Tawney, another grad student, and I interviewed him one afternoon. We lingered so long that he finally pulled out a flask and took a long pull of—whiskey? We learned how eager students overstaying their welcome can drive even a Zen master to a drink.

The next day, I had an individual conference with Gary. Numb with anxiety, I unfolded the "Blue Spot" poem and spread it on the desk.

And after reading the poem, Gary Snyder gently said . . .

"'Yanked off his tail' sounds so violent." He went on to explain an essential principle about poetry and all writing: Each word must help create a consistent whole. Tone, in the literary sense, is like the musical key of a song, with minor or major shadings. Wrong notes jar the listener. Harmony pleases.

When Gary pointed out this one word, "yanked," I suddenly understood his point, in a satori moment. It clearly did not fit the rest of the poem. I changed the word to "snipped," and the poem was corrected. I learned how to curate words more carefully, and in poetry, every single word counts.

Gary gave me another tip: Use Anglo-Saxon words when possible. What fun English-speaking poets have had since Geoffrey Chaucer began writing in the vernacular English rather than the literary language of Latin. English speakers have a zillion high culture and low culture jargons, dialects, popular culture references, and slangs. So, selecting words, and words consistent with each other, can be a challenge. Their histories matter.

London peasants' patios provide 83% of the most common thousand words in English, and "yank" is one of them. It is one-syllable, direct, and vivid. It can be said quickly, just like the abrupt action it represents. Other Anglo-Saxon words include similarly colorful and efficient terms like ax, cup, door, gold, bang, marsh, rain, rat, rock, yolk, and snip. "Snip" is Old English, and also it imitates the sound it represents, so it is a double bonus point word for my poem. Also, the music of scissors is less alarming than the whack of an ax. "Snip" fits my tender poem much better than, say, "excise," a Latin-derived word, or another, "truncate."

Words ending with "sion" or "tion" come from the Roman invasion of Britain, an imperialist intrusion in many ways. Latinate words include words like "cognition," "education," circumlocution," "deviation," and "obfuscation." Latinate words are tongue-twisters and slow down a poem's momentum. In some cases, this may be the poet's intent, but the Latin-based vocabulary reads like a manual, not a song.

Gary's nudge to consider each word carefully led me to look at more word histories, especially from Indigenous American heritages. His college thesis was about Indigenous peoples (*The Old Ways*), he worked with Indigenous loggers in California, and he had profound respect for the first peoples of the American continents. In the northeastern United States, early European sailors met, mostly, Algonquin speakers, so moccasin, toboggan, moose, terrapin, and other borrowed words are now standard English.

To honor my Indigenous relatives and histories, I sometimes use Lenape and Cherokee terms. I was lucky to study Cherokee with Andy Girty, a native speaker, and Maura Garcia. A word or phrase from another language can be important to a poem.

I learned so much after Gary spoke gently about my error. Without lecturing, the sage also helped me understand that a piece of writing should be one unbroken whole. A conscientious writers sands smooth the piece of writing as though they were making a wooden ax handle. Graphic language, obscenities, mild cuss words, exclamations, or euphemisms—these all signal whether the poet locates a poem in the parlor, the tavern, or the toilet. Any irregularity will stick out.

During my meeting with Gary that afternoon so long ago, I hardly spoke, but I hung on his every word. He did not resort to his flask during that afternoon one-on-one, so perhaps our session was not overly tedious. "Mindful" was not a term in those days, but I heard what he said. I thought about it for days—for decades. The invisible connotations of words have importance along with the denotations—and the wise poet listens to the silences among the notes.

Jim Natal

Oil and Water

THE OIL AND WATER of my life. That's how I used to describe the surface tension separating my poetry and my corporate career with the National Football League. I was hired as a freelance copywriter by NFL Properties Creative Services in Los Angeles in May of 1978. Almost exactly 25 years later I held an executive editor title when the League decided to close the LA office in 2003.

We were kind of a stealth operation out on the West Coast. While the League's main administrative and marketing functions were headquartered on Park Avenue in New York, our office was responsible for creative content: NFL books, magazines, game programs (including for the Super Bowl), along with anything requiring League-sanctioned design, such as team uniforms and licensed merchandise. At the time, the NFL ranked second in international sales of officially licensed merchandise behind only the Walt Disney Company; the NFL is now thirteenth globally with Disney still on top.

Our small office was staffed with sportswriters, graphic designers, and production specialists—the most talented team I've ever been on. I was the odd duck because although I could write statistic-laden sports stories and player profiles, I also could write licensing and League promotional copy. My role developed into serving as the liaison between our L.A. creative group, the New York marketing staff, and NFL corporate clients and their assorted outside agencies. I was as close to a "suit" as anyone in our office ever got. In other words, it was a dream gig, with occasional travel to Manhattan, visits to corporate clients, and trips to the Super Bowl every year. So, you may be asking, where's the "but"? And where does poetry fit in? Let me answer with poetic compression: the corporate pressure of the job was killing my soul and poetry saved it.

Though I was born in Chicago, my sensibilities were shaped on the shores of Lake Michigan near what is now Indiana Dunes National Park.

My family spent a couple of summers there, then became year-round residents for four years in the late 1950s, with my father commuting to his office in Chicago. Nature entered my life in a formative way among those beaches and dunes, especially in the quiet seasons, fall through spring when the summer homes that lined the beach road stood empty. I was a loner kid. Walking the shoreline among the drifts and dune grass, I began to see natural connections, think in metaphors, to make leaps in my mind that I didn't yet recognize as the essence of poetry. I vaguely remember winning a writing award in elementary school for a description of the beach in winter.

My father's job necessitated a move back to Chicago but that beach environment came with me, was grafted to me as if a fruiting branch. It's there still, provides a refuge, safe passage, and spirit nourishment like the poetry that later gave solace.

I wake up every morning to a watercolor of the low dunes leading to Lake Michigan that my mother bought at a local beach town art fair when I was eight or nine. I used it as the cover image of my first full-length poetry collection, *In the Bee Trees*, which includes a number of poems relating to that sacred time.

[Cut to classic film montage of calendar pages drifting down like autumn leaves.] College at William & Mary and Ohio State; an early marriage; a divorce; attempts to eke out an existence as a freelance writer first in Chicago, then in Santa Fe, and finally Los Angeles in 1976. A number of odd hires came and went, including brief tours of duty as a MasterCard rep and neighborhood restaurant chef before yellow brick serendipity led me to the NFL. The birth of a daughter; another divorce; my steady albeit high-stress position. Life, as the saying goes, got in the way of my writing like a downfield blocker.

F. Scott Fitzgerald's bromide about there being no second acts in American lives was weighing on my mind when poetry quietly slipped into bed with me again while I was working for the NFL. I say "again" because I had written a few dozen poems in high school and in college charged by the songs of Leonard Cohen, Bob Dylan, and Joni Mitchell, even put together a chapbook in my senior year at OSU that I illustrated using a variety of printmaking techniques. My father, normally supportive, took me aside one day to tell me that poetry was a stage everyone went through and would pass, and that I should consider pursuing something else. In a strictly financial sense, he was right. I now wonder (but never asked) if it was a stage *he* went through.

Speaking of my father, he was an avid football fan. Back when there were two competing pro football leagues, the NFL and AFL, he had a pair of TVs stacked on top of one another so he could watch the televised games of both leagues at the same time. I played organized football in elementary school, varsity in high school, and intramural in college and have a bad shoulder and a cleat scar on my shin to prove it.

Trying to allay my sinking in that corporate sea in the mid-1990s, I sought release in martial arts, 10K races, cooking. I surprised myself by turning to poems for comfort, which rekindled an urge to write. An image just occurred to me: I was the tube and poetry was the toothpaste; my NFL work life provided the hard squeeze to bring it out. I was determined not to squander the second chance I got, the return of my poetry muse.

I began going to readings. After one of those—an all-star event featuring Philip Levine, Ed Hirsch, and Garrett Hongo at the late, lamented Midnight Special Books in Santa Monica—I picked up a flyer for the store's regular Saturday afternoon poetry workshop. I'm not normally a "joiner" but I decided to try a session. I ended up attending for more than two years, rarely missing a Saturday gathering. Now, going on twenty-five years later, I still workshop regularly with some of those same poets and our second group anthology will be published in 2025.

Meanwhile, back in the office, I felt like one of those cartoon characters with one foot on each of two train rails that suddenly split in different directions. Business meetings and projects competed with literary readings and open mic nights. Then the NFLs L.A. office was shut down and an opportunity presented itself to enroll in the Antioch MFA in Creative Writing program. I had always wanted to go. However, the program's low-residency format required two weeks in person on campus in December, which was Super Bowl crunch time at work. Put that decision to attend in the "win" column.

Since then, I've taught creative writing, curated and run multi-year reading series and literary events, and co-founded an indie press publishing primarily poetry. My sixth full-length poetry collection is forthcoming. I've had the pleasure of interviewing dozens of major writers and poets and given countless readings. RE poetry readings: I rarely get nervous presenting my work no matter the venue. After getting up in front of a hotel ballroom full of impassive beer executives and distributors to pitch a multi-million-dollar NFL partnership, a poetry audience is the proverbial walk in the ballpark. Both endeavors, though, are in their way full-contact sports.

I still do occasionally ponder why I chose poetry or poetry chose me, why I toil at that form of self-expression. I've tried short fiction, written a manuscript of a novel that currently resides in a drawer. I always wanted to paint like Bonnard or Rothko, sing and play guitar like Bruce Springsteen. But, instead, I was gifted poetry in all its forms and have come to marvel at its shrewd and vexing balance of complexity and simplicity, its precision of word and craft, its power to work in your head beyond and between the lines confined to the page, and its ability to express the inexpressible with near physical impact.

Still, if I had to choose a specific moment on my journey, it would be late one summer night on the south side of Chicago. There's me as a boy looking out my bedroom window at branches backlit by streetlights and feeling the spark, jolt, flow—call it what you will. That first real poem I was inspired to write is long lost, but I still remember the opening line: "Trees and shadows of trees . . ."

Elaine Equi

Square One

I AM A SPORADIC WRITER. I have a need to go away and come back. I'll write three or four poems, and then pleased with myself, take off for weeks, even a month or more, until I feel something is missing from my life—that feeling only writing a poem can provide.

Okay, so now I'm ready to sit down and write again, but it's not that easy. Inevitably, everything I write sounds terrible. I have trouble coming up with a single interesting line. Even though I've published several books, I find myself back at square one—starting over.

It's not actually a bad place to be, and I rather enjoy (sort of) the process of feeling my way back into looking at language from the inside. I have a few simple tricks and techniques that help me; I'm hoping you may also find them of use.

Make A Clearing

For me, an essential part of writing is to make a clearing,

first in my mind, then on the page,
so words can be seen, heard, taste-tested.

A clear ring like one of those pristine sound booths
that will allow the words to resonate.

White space is important.

What's not said can be as important, possibly more important, than what is.

There are already so many texts, messages, words directed at us each day.
Every inch, every surface, seems covered in words.

But even words need room to breathe—and breed.

Recently, I was delighted when a poet I highly respect said,
"If I want to write, I need lots of time to do nothing. Space out. Sit and stare."

When I feel inundated by language, I like to take the scenic route and escape into a more visual mode of thought.

I like to take photographs and study paintings. As I say in one aphorism, "Pictures can cure us of words."

For someone else, it might be music or nature or yoga or all of the above.

The point is to take a moment to cleanse your literary palate so you can return to words refreshed and eager to hear what they have to say.

Choose A Word

Or let it choose you.

A single word can be a powerful prompt.

When teaching, I often used to start the semester with this assignment: write a poem that comes from a single word. A word you love. A word you hate. A word you chose at random from the dictionary. It's surprising how evocative one word can be.

You can delve into all the personal associations the word has for you.
You can look up its etymology and trace its history.
You can approach it sonically—riffing off the sounds of its letters and components, amplifying them with alliteration and rhyme.

One variation that especially appeals to me is to write a poem using the chosen word in almost every line. Since we're normally discouraged in creative writing classes from repeating the same word twice in a poem, it's fun to give yourself the freedom to do the complete opposite.

By way of example, here's a short poem of mine about "weird," a word I like very much and use to describe all kinds of things—good and bad.

Ode To Weird

Emily Dickinson was weird.
Fernando Pessoa was definitely weird.

All poets are weird
even when their poems
try to appear normal.

Macbeth's weird sisters
stirring up trouble's
unsavory soup:

"Just be yourself
and you'll be king."

Weird always wins and loses in the end.

Keep A Fragment Diary

The beauty of the fragment is its detachment and immediacy.

A fragment diary is just what it sounds like—a collection of scraps of language and stray lines or images that intrigue you and make your mind do a double take. It is also the record of a day or a week or a month in your life told in a unique style of shorthand.

The idea for keeping such a journal came out of a Lit Seminar I was teaching called The Minimalist Mystique. In it, we'd read all kinds of short (mostly poetry) texts and discuss what made them work so well. In addition to critical responses, I'd ask students to engage with some formal aspect of what we were studying. When we read Basho and Issa, they wrote haiku and haibun. When we read *Tender Buttons* and *Paris Spleen*, they wrote prose poems. When we read the Objectivists, they wrote serial poems. So when we read *7 Greeks*, Guy Davenport's marvelous translations of ancient Greek poets and philosophers such as Sappho, Herakleitos, and Diogenes, we wrote in fragments.

Even if these texts were not originally written as fragments, the way we experience them today is piecemeal and riddled with gaps. I wanted us to immerse ourselves in that spare, intermittent pattern of thought. Instead of waiting hundreds of years for time to edit and erase our words, we'd do it ourselves.

Thanks to the Futurists, along with Eliot, Pound, H.D., and a host of other modernists, no one would question the validity and relevance of this mode of expression. Also, trained as we are by Twitter and other forms of social media, it's quite natural for us to condense our words.

What I find most appealing about the fragment diary is that it's a journal where none of your thoughts ever has to be finished–a catalog and celebration of incomplete things. I can't tell you how many times I've thought a good beginning in a book, movie, or essay is destroyed by a tedious middle or forced over-the-top ending. I guess who would want to buy a ticket to see just the great beginning of a movie, although I might actually be that person.

I love that the poet Larry Fagin has a book called *Complete Fragments*. It's so perfectly, perversely funny.

Of course, I do like to write things where I have to struggle to develop an idea over time. But that is a task for when I'm feeling more confident. When I find myself back at Square One, I keep a fragment diary to ease me back into the flow of words. I think of it an interim step, on the way to writing—on the way to language as Heidegger says.

I will end here with another short poem of mine collaged from different entries in one of my fragment diaries.

Crayon

Weather colors the day.

Breath inflates our aches.

Bobbing along the surface.

Why must I always

finish my sentences?

It's as if
            and now can't stop.

Phillip Lopate

The Poetry Years

THOUGH I AM KNOWN TODAY mostly as an essayist, occasionally as a fiction writer, for about fifteen years I wrote poetry. I published poems in countless little magazines, gave readings all over, earned a living of sorts as a poet in the schools, teaching the art to children, and put out two collections: the first in 1972, the second in 1976. When I look back at those years during which poetry formed such an important part of my identity, I am tempted to rub my eyes, as though recalling a time when I ran off and joined the circus; yet at the time it seemed a logical enough pursuit.

How had I started writing poetry in the first place? I can honestly say I had no ambitions to be a poet when I was younger. True, in elementary school I was by default the class poet, just as there was a boy who drew horses well and another boy who ran the fastest at Field Day. When Thanksgiving approached, I would be expected to craft a few stanzas about the pilgrims' feast. In junior high I wrote several tortured poems under the influence of the Beats. But by high school I had forsaken poetry for prose: if I had any literary ambitions, it was to be a novelist.

In college, joining the literary circle around *Columbia Review*, I befriended a number of emerging poets, including Jonathan Cott and Ron Padgett. Jonathan was my best friend and was highly cultivated, drawn to such serious, demanding authors as Holderlin, Lowell, Roethke. The Oklahoma-born Padgett and I had heard of each other before ever meeting, circling each other like gunfighters; he had even put the word out that he was going to break my butt. Of course, when we finally met the conversation was amicable and respectful. Padgett had precociously started a poetry magazine back in high school, writing to poets he admired for contributions; and he came to New York to attend Columbia as part of a Tulsa émigré gang who affixed themselves immediately to the New York School of Poetry. I settled for becoming a hanger-on in the poetry scene, with entrée provided by Ron Padgett, all of us worshipping at the shrine of Koch, Frank O'Hara and John Ashbery. The one whose poetry appealed to me most in that period was O'Hara, partly because of his unapologetically urban, movie-mad sensibility, partly because of his doctrine of Personalism. His example gave casual permission to construct a poem out of anything at hand, from a friend's remark to a movie star's collapse to a headline or honking car or sudden mood change.

Just as there was a *politique des auteurs* among film buffs, so a sort of *politque des poètes* existed, with battle lines drawn between the more Establishment-respected and prize-winning poets of the day, such as Robert Lowell, Richard Wilbur, John Berryman, Elizabeth Bishop, Richard Eberhart, Anthony Hecht, Anne Sexton, and so on, and the New York School, who drew their inspiration from the French modernist poets and the painting of Willem de Kooning, Jackson Pollock, Larry Rivers, Jane Freilicher, etc. Koch's poem "Fresh Air" was a manifesto against everything solemn, high-minded, ethically worrying—"academic," in a word—and called for a poetics of sensuous, experimental linguistic play. Of course, these divisions grew fuzzier the closer you examined the matter: Koch himself taught in the academy, as Ashbery later would, and who could be wittier or more linguistically playful than Wilbur? But there was still this seeming antagonism between opposing teams, the one (the "established" poets) using poetry as a criticism of life, the other (the New York School) as a celebration of art. I remember visiting second-generation New York School poet Ted Berrigan in his East Village pad, and being told by him that he never mixed life with art. Art came from art, he said, not life. Anyone reading Ted's heart-breaking, autobiographical *Sonnets* would be hard-pressed to concur with his assertion; but that was at least the party line.

When I first began dipping into the poetry of Berryman, Lowell, Bishop, Sexton and Sylvia Plath, I felt guilty, like a Catholic reading books on the Index, and even guiltier for liking them so much. In the last analysis, what I took from my days as a New York Poetry School fellow-traveler was less aesthetic than social. I had the privilege to watch the way a lively poetry scene mushroomed at St. Marks' Church on the Bouwerie, in the East Village, under the nurturance of Anne Waldman. This was the closest I would ever come to the Banquet Years, and though I have always considered myself a literary loner, it gave me a glimpse of how a circle, a generation, a movement, a bohemia functioned. I accepted the poets' generous invitations to parties, to passed joints, to publications in mimeo magazines, to friendships and acquaintanceships. What they made of me I have no idea. I lived way uptown, at the northern end of Manhattan above the Cloisters: one time I threw a party and invited the St. Mark's crowd to it, though they seemed wary ever of venturing above 14th Street. They arrived late, having brought with them on the A train enough reading matter for an ocean crossing, and immediately headed for the bedroom to get stoned, ignoring my other literary friends in the living room. But if the St. Marks poets were insular, they were also warmly loyal. I was fascinated by the way they supported each other. I once asked Ron Padgett how he and Ted Berrigan critiqued one another's poems. "I just say, 'That's totally terrific, Ted,' and when I show him mine he says 'That's totally terrific' to me." Whether this was actually true I have my doubts, but the lesson seemed to be that critical fussiness was passé. As eye-opening as all this was, it did not necessarily make me want to be a poet. That came about another way.

Living on the brink of poverty, I was looking for some freelance editorial work (often a euphemism for ghostwriting, which I did extensively during this period), when I came upon a notice requesting readers to help edit a new poetry anthology. Reading was one thing I felt sure I could do; I did very little else. So, I answered the ad and was summoned to a noon interview at the home of one Hy Sobiloff. He, often referred to in those days as "the businessman-poet," was a wealthy investor and venture capitalist who lived in a very tony townhouse on East 77th Street in the Upper East Side. Sobiloff explained the nature of the project, which was to revise the immensely popular poetry anthologies that had been edited by his late friend Oscar Williams. I was happy to tell him my mother had read aloud from them to us as children such favorites as Alfred Noyes' The Highwayman. Poetically, you might say, Oscar Williams' anthologies were mother's-milk to me. Sobiloff gruffly cut me off, saying the point was that they needed to be updated. He had undertaken the chore as an act of devotion to a friend who'd passed away. He pointed to several precipitously tall stacks of poetry books on French Empire chairs and said, "I know all this stuff cold but I can't be bothered to go through 'em. The interview lasted ten minutes at most. He seemed satisfied; we agreed on a salary, and I took away a few shopping bags full of books.

I had now to educate myself as quickly as possible in the English and American poetic canon. I was overwhelmed by the vast amounts of poetry I would have to absorb, but I began by plowing through the original Williams anthologies. I quickly saw that Oscar Williams had put his friend Hy in the books, as he had his wife Gene Derwood and himself, though their verse hardly seemed in the same league with Keats and Whitman. Sobiloff, I learned, was philanthropically active, and a heavy supporter of poetry societies and magazines

Shortly after beginning the job, I learned I was not the only poetry reader; Sobiloff had hired two others, like a gambler placing bets across the board. At first, he kept us strictly separate; but in time I was able to contact them, and consolidate my position as First Reader, *primer ante pares*, by offering to coordinate the project for a slightly higher fee. He appreciated my ruthlessness, I think.

Believe me, I had no intention of cutting corners. My work schedule consisted of reading four poetry books a day minimum. Most of them came from the library, some from used book stores—our boss had given us permission to augment his limited stock, and I saved the receipts for him. I would wake up and eat breakfast while starting on the first, get dressed, finish reading the book, take some notes about possible selections and go off for a walk with a bag lunch around noontime, often ending on a bench in Riverside Park (my wife and I had by this time moved down from Inwood to West 104th Street, near Columbia), where I would read a second book and begin paging through a third . . . So I would give it a rest, then turn to book four in the late afternoon, and maybe book five that evening, if I had anything left in me. Over-stuffed like a goose for the manufacture of *foie gras*, I had no choice but to secrete my own poems. So mentally swamped with the elevated lyrical language of others, out of sheer defensive survival I needed to have my say.

Two other factors, besides the anthology reader gig, sparked my entry into poetry in the years I am describing, 1967–69: the political upheaval of the anti-war movement. Close to Columbia University, I got swept up in the 1968 student revolt and reentered my old Alma Mater as a trouble-making alumnus. Just as I had been a hanger-on at the New York School of Poetry scene, so now I became a fellow-traveler of the New Left, participating in demonstrations, political meetings and study groups, reading Marxist texts along with all the poetry. I never felt entirely comfortable with the posture of radicalism, nor could I embrace deep-down the hope of making revolution, being an ex-scholarship kid from the ghetto still trying to claw my way into the middle class.

Meanwhile, my first novel had not found a publisher; I was unable to take defeat in stride and start on a second one. Writing novels requires a calm, settled, bourgeois existence, and the payoff is deferred for years. The fragmentation I felt so painfully in those days would not permit me to submerge myself again in a prolonged alternate dream-narrative. I needed a form I could turn to with quicker results, snatching a few hours here and there from a patched-together freelance existence and the emotional confusion of whether to leave or stay. Hence, poetry.

My first poems seemed to emerge from a personal conjugal dilemma. These poems now strike me as tentative and hypocritical, the way a couple in their last stage bullshits during marriage counseling while secretly eyeing the exit. Formally, I was feeling my way into poetry at the same time I was feeling my way out of the marriage. Incidentally, I have always derived poetic inspiration from breakups.

I had decided to leave New York for California, the promised land of youth culture. Before I decamped, I turned in my lists of recommendations for the updated anthologies. I had wanted the collections to seem less stuffy, less "academic," so I added Bessie Smith and Bob Dylan lyrics, and Native American chants, and a slew of Black poets, and of course increased the selections of the New York School poets, and F. T. Prince, John Wheelwright, Robert Creeley, George Oppen, Ed Dorn and Allen Ginsberg, among others. Sobiloff looked them over without a word. Years later, when the revised anthologies appeared, I had a hard time finding any evidence of my labors. But the job had served its purpose: it had given me a condensed poetic education.

•

The poets who influenced me the most at the beginning of my poetic career were William Carlos Williams, Frank O'Hara, Pablo Neruda, Vladimir Mayakovsky, and Randall Jarrell. I was happy to purloin Williams' three-line stanzas or O'Hara's splattering of words across the page; to imitate Mayakovsky's mock-megalomaniac outbursts, Neruda's surreal inventories or the loquacity of late Jarrell. Later on, I would fall in love with the dramatic monologues at the back of Pasternak's Doctor Zhivago, and Cavafy's deceptively simple lyrics and history poems, and Pavese's Hard Labor, with its dense materialist details of quotidian working-class life.

I was searching for something that made me happy whenever I found it, but I still didn't know how to characterize it. Though I had been a fan of Neruda's, when I attended a reading of his at the 92nd Street Y, he put me off with his hammy, Stalin Prize delivery. It was another Chilean poet, Nicanor Parra, who crystallized for me what I was looking for, with his collection *Poems and Anti-Poems*. This taste for "anti-poetry," for grubby reality, is addressed by Wallace Stevens in his preface to the 1934 Collected Poems by William Carlos Williams, when he describes Williams as someone for whom "the anti-poetic is that truth, that reality to which all of us are forever fleeing." I was drawn to the antipoetic for a number of reasons. First, my training had been in fiction, and I was still very charmed by the sound of conversational prose. Though literary critics might disparage a poem as being "chopped-up prose," that was insufficient to condemn it in my eyes. Quite the contrary: it interested me, perversely, to see how far one could go in that direction and still get away with it. I also found it attractive when poets employed a complex syntax that took a whole stanza or sonnet to uncoil—more so than a row of staccato end-stopped lines. A storyteller at heart, I continued to like narrative. Some of Parra's and Cavafy's narrative situations were like little short stories: a room, a memory, a pickup.

Yes, I was rebelling against the lingering idea that poems should contain words or emotions that were suitably "poetic"—the beauties of nature, flowers, finches, rapture, elevated sentiment; I was drawn to a more sardonic poetry that would traffic in mundane commercial objects, business terms, legalese, you name it. It pleased me beyond measure to be able to use a word like "bicameral" in a poem on Allende. A city rat, I had no command of the names of flora and fauna, and needed to stake my claim with vocabulary that would verge on the prosaic and anti-romantic.

Finally, being poetically self-taught and, despite having read books on prosody from Saintsbury to Hollander, finding that very little of it stuck to me, never able to master my quantities, meters and values, never having gone to graduate school to study poetry, I still composed poems largely intuitively, on the basis of what rhythms or combinations "sounded right" to my ear. Essentially I was trying to turn a limitation (my ignorance) into a strength (my preference for the anti-poetic).

To some degree, I was taking permission from the era's looser standards. The 1960s allowed for a wide open, pluralistic (some would say amateurish) poetics. The ascendance of the oral, first-word-best-word "rap" through the Beats and black activist poets such as Gil Scott Heron and the Last Poets, the cultural enthronement of rock troubadours, the proliferation of open readings and mimeo magazines, the promotion of children's poetry and ethnopoetics, all contributed to the idea that anyone could write poetry or had the right to call oneself a poet. I suppose I sneaked in under that umbrella.

•

A key determinant for me during these years was becoming friends with the poet Bill Zavatsky, a friendship I am happy to say has lasted forty years. Zavatsky is a large-hearted, open, funny man and a very fine poet, as well as a capable jazz pianist. When I first met him around 1968, he was writing ebullient verse that ran arpeggios in all directions. Robert Lowell once commented that he found it hard to "people" his poems. I, with my fiction background and interest in psychological cul-de-sacs, found that part relatively easy; my poetic struggles were on another plane. In any case, Zavatsky was drawn to what I was doing, and he encouraged me to keep writing situational, reality-based poems.

Zavatsky had recently gotten an MFA in poetry-writing at Columbia, where he'd studied with Stanley Kunitz and Harvey Shapiro, and he introduced me to a circle of young Kunitz/Shapiro trained poets, which included Hugh Seidman, Mark Rudman and Louise Gluck, who hung out at the West End Bar and other venues in Morningside Heights. Soon, I was participating in their open readings, and learning from them. Through them I became familiar with another poetic model, the Objectivists (George Oppen, Louis Zukofsky and Carl Rakosi), and their younger allies, Harvey Shapiro, Armand Schwerner and David Ignatow. I was particularly taken with the hard-bitten, wry, tight urban lyrics of Shapiro and Ignatow. Certain of my poems seem to have come directly out of an attempt to write like them. But the poet in the Objectivist orbit who came to affect me most was Charles Reznikoff. He was still around then, though elderly, and had been rediscovered, championed by younger poets, who were as moved by his example of humility and non-careerism as by his spare, tender poems.

•

Two other, nonliterary influences on my poetry during that time deserve mention. The first was psychotherapy. I was seeing a Jungian psychologist named George Romney, a Cuban émigré who smoked cigarillos and had wavy black hair and an infectious laugh; it became my secret goal to provoke that laugh of his as often as possible in sessions. I would tell him about my experiences, and sometimes in the midst of relating them they would cohere into a kind of improvised poem, which would make him chuckle and which I would then go home and try to write down. In this way, my long poem, "The Blue Pants," came about. George also frequently asked me, as therapists are wont to do, what I was feeling in the moment, directing my attention to the emotion physiologically manifesting and gurgling in my body. Out of this practice of attempting to pin down emotional states came poems such as "Numbness," "Not Sadness Which Is Always There," and "Clearing a Space." The very ambition to write poems based in the present moment—to open myself to the here-and-now, as it were—derived from techniques I had been learning in psychotherapy.

The second crucial nonliterary influence on my poetry was teaching inner-city children and teenagers. I worked as a poet-in-the-schools for over a dozen years, first helping high school dropouts in East Harlem get their equivalency degree, then directing a program for Teachers & Writers Collaborative at P.S. 75 in the Upper West Side of Manhattan. Poems such as "Satin Doll" and"Rumors" (along with my first published prose book, *Being With Children*), resulted from that work experience, which brought me closer to my own memories of childhood and early adolescence.

Teaching kids grew partly out of a desire to be socially useful: to put my politics into practice. I was also looking for ways to incorporate my politics into my poetry. In one case, I had been leafing through a picture book of Cuban revolutionary art, and I came upon a propaganda poster with the title "Solidarity with Mozambique," and wondered how on earth I could ever feel my way into bonding with a struggle that seemed so far away and so abstract. I began writing about daily occurrences in New York City, then tried to reach, by concentric circles leading farther and farther away from myself, the rebels in Mozambique. (Not that I ever convincingly made it.)

Around 1977, I started writing personal essays and also went back to longer fiction. I see in retrospect the way I was handling the same material, the same themes, in poetry and prose. "The Second Marriage" reads like a poem-précis of the novella by the same title. A protest against "the bullying urge to feel" can be found in "Numbness" and the essay "Against Joie de Vivre." "Secrets, Rehearsals" was like a dry run for my essay, "The Story of My Father." The single person learning to be alone is a theme sounded in many of these poems no less than in the prose that makes up my first essay collection, *Bachelorhood*.

To go back to 1972: I had been amassing sufficient poems for a first collection when a printer based in Northampton approached me and offered to put them out in a chapbook. The plan was for me to spend the month of August at his print shop, learning to operate a letter press and assisting in the production of the book, to be entitled *The Eyes Don't Always Want to Stay Open.* When I arrived in Northampton, however, I discovered that the printer and his wife were going through a messy divorce, and he was temporarily closing the business while they sorted out the division of conjugal assets. I was welcome, he said, to stay in their house for the month of August, now that it had been vacated by both husband and wife, who had moved in with their new lovers. I was miserably lonely and felt foolish and hollow. But as it happened, an elderly woman neighbor, highly cultivated, befriended me. She knew how to operate the letter press. So we set in type exactly one of my poems, the paranoid epistle "We Who Are Your Closest Friends," as a broadside. (Anne Lamott, to my surprise, included this poem in her popular writing manual, *Bird by Bird,* thus bringing it to thousands of readers it would otherwise not have reached).

•

What remains to be told is how or why I gave up writing poetry. There is a simple answer and a complicated one. First the simple one: in 1980, I moved to Houston, Texas, to teach at the University of Houston. I had been recruited as the creative writing program's first prose writer, on the basis of my memoir about teaching, *Being with Children,* my novel *Confessions of Summer* and my soon-to-be-released personal essay collection, *Bachelorhood.* If in New York I had been accepted as a poet, such was not the case in Houston. I was not permitted to teach poetry courses, in spite of having published two books' worth.

A higher, "purer" standard of what it took to be a poet seemed to reign in that corner of academia, based partly on the possession of an MFA credential, and partly on the networking of the professional poetry world. I got a real taste of the way that poetry guild mentality operated: the mentoring and bestowal of the blessing on a chosen few acolytes, whose books would then be recommended for publication. I knew I'd never gotten a message from on high: I did not fit that bill. My sense of myself as a poet began to shrivel up.

Moreover, I could never have been deterred from writing poetry if my Houston colleagues' judgment had not gibed with something already inside me, some insecure spot that made me feel that, on some level, I was an imposter. It had been a good long run, but it was time to stop pretending I was a poet.

Around 1983, I drifted away from writing poems, the only exceptions being the occasional birthday ode or the email poems I would exchange with my daughter when I was away, to encourage her to send me her own poems. But recently, when offered the chance to have these two earlier collections reprinted, along with any additional poems that were not included in them, I found myself going through this material and—liking much of it. As I retyped individual poems in my computer, I would change phrases, sharpen a rhythm, clarify an idea. I remembered how much fun it was to write poems, how happily engaged I could be for hours in tiny adjustments. Suddenly, I couldn't understand why I had given it up.

Will I take up the practice again? I certainly hope so. I'm well aware that established prose writers often publish their hobby-ish poems out of vanity. I would like to think there is more going on here in this collection: the urge to give pleasure to new readers. When I read my old poems today, it strikes me with a mixture of regret and relief that I am no longer the person who wrote them. Some are obviously young man's poems, and their callow hungers embarrass me now. Yet, I cannot help finding that younger self touching, and in any case, revealing. It is not for me, finally, to judge them as poems. I will leave that up to you.

R. L. Stine

Say yes to things you meet.
You don't know where they will lead.

An Interview by Sandy McIntosh

I WAS A VERY SHY and very fearful kid, afraid of a lot of things, and I think maybe that's why I enjoyed writing so much. I started writing when I was nine. I dragged a typewriter into my room, and I'd be typing all afternoon, typing out joke books and little funny stories and things, but I don't know why I enjoyed it so much. My parents didn't understand it at all. My mother would stand outside my bedroom door and say, "What's wrong with you? Stop typing, go outside and play."

Go outside? Worst advice I ever got right. "Stop typing and go play."

I'd say, "It's boring out there, boring," and I'd type, type, type.

In college at Ohio State, I edited the humor magazine, *The Sundial.* Every college had a humor magazine in those days, and I edited it for three years. That's all I did. I just did that magazine, and it paid my way to New York from Ohio.

In those days, I thought, if you wanted to be a writer you had to live in New York. I didn't know you had a choice. So, I packed up and moved to Greenwich Village from Columbus.

When I began, I wrote everything. I've written about forty joke books for kids and published a humor magazine called *Bananas* for ten years. Before we started the scary books. I wrote coloring books. I wrote *Mighty Mouse* coloring books. It'd be one line to write at the bottom of the page. I wrote for Bazooka Joe, the comics that came with the bubble gum. I was never in the army, never handled a gun, but I wrote *G.I. Joe* books.

·

I never planned to write scary stories. It wasn't even my idea to be scary.

I just wanted to be funny; that's all I cared about, and I thought, as I was writing for my humor magazine, that that was my life's dream.

When that ended, I figured I would coast the rest of my life. I had no idea what was in store for me. Every project I took up after that seemed to come to me as an accident—one accident after another—but I always said yes to each. I don't give much advice to younger writers except to tell them to say yes to things they meet because you don't know where they will lead.

For instance, I was having lunch with a friend who was a publisher at Scholastic. When she arrived, she was angry. She had fought with an author who wrote teen horror novels. She told me she'd never work with him again. Then she looked at me and said, "You know, you could write a good teen horror novel."

"How?"

"It's simple: Go home and write a book called *Blind Date*."

I thought about it. I had no idea what a teen novel was, but she had given me the title. So, without knowing anything about it, I said yes to her because I always said yes to everything.

After lunch, I ran to the bookstore to see what teen novels were. I bought books written by Lois Duncan and Christopher Pike, among others—there were many authors writing teen horror in the late eighties—because I wanted to see what they were doing and what a teen horror novel was! After I read them, I started right in and wrote *Blind Date*. The title was enough to get me to write the book.

Well, it was published, and *Blind Date* became the number one bestseller!

Nothing I had written before had ever been on that list. I kept going back and writing more in the same genre. A year later, I published another, *Twisted*, which also became the number one bestseller.

At that point, I thought, "Forget the funny stuff. I'm going to be scary from now on." And I've been scary ever since.

•

When you think of it, there's a close connection between humor and horror. For instance, when you go up behind somebody, you go BOOM! What's the first thing they do? They gasp, right? And then they laugh. People have the same visceral reaction to both. I think horror is funny.

Horror makes me laugh. I mean, the reaction is just very close. And I think that is why it was easy for me to switch over.

I also include a lot of humor in scary books, especially in the *Goosebumps* stories. Humor is important because I don't want these stories to be too frightening for kids.

I want to give them a release from the tension. If the story gets too intense, I throw in something funny.

•

I've been writing *Goosebumps* for thirty-three years now. One after the other. I just finished one last week. And I still look forward to coming up with new finishes, new chapter endings, meeting new challenges, solving new problems.

Despite whatever is going on, whatever turmoil might be going on behind the scenes, I write every day. I'm a machine. I write from 10:00 AM to 1:00 PM every day. I have a lot of publishing contracts with deadlines, and to meet those, I must turn out so much every day.

Those are the best hours of my day.

People may think that after thirty years of writing this stuff, it's easier. They say, "Oh, he found the formula." But my question is: What's the formula? I wish someone would tell me.

In fact, after thirty years, trying to think of something you haven't done before is a lot harder, a lot more challenging. For instance, all my chapter endings are cliffhangers. I don't want to repeat myself. I want to come up with something that I haven't done before. If I knew the formula, I'd probably get bored. Then, I'd ask ChatGPT to write the books, and I think that would be the end.

I have publicists. I have a wonderful full-time publicist who was publicity director at Scholastic for thirteen years. I also have publicists at all the different publishers that publish my books.

I manage my own social media, including Facebook, X, and Instagram. I enjoy that part.

•

People who want to write don't need advice. They don't need somebody telling them, "Read a lot and write every day." They're already doing that. Real writers, I think they're like me, they know. That's what they want to do.

But I'm often on author panels, and every time, some author will get up and say, "Writing is hard. I have to lock my kids in the garage, so I have time to write. Writing is just so hard!"

But if you go into writing thinking it's hard, it will be hard for you. But if you adjust your thinking, and you realize with writing you're accepting a real, worthwhile challenge, you suddenly find yourself having a great time. Wow! No heavy lifting, right? No hard hat, no nothing. It's going to be a lot more fun. You're creating a world. You're developing people. You're sitting there making up your whole universe. It makes writing a lot easier.

David St. John

Ellen Bass

Amber
Flora Thomas

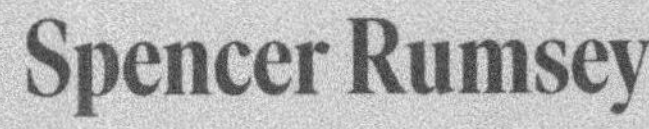

Spencer Rumsey

Eileen R. Tabios

Stephen Paul Miller

Liane Strauss

David St. John

You Can't Judge a Book

> Oh can't you see
> Oh you misjudged me
> I look like a farmer but
> I'm a lover
> Can't judge a book
> By looking at the cover
>
> —Bo Diddley

AUTHORS ARE OFTEN EITHER famously disappointed by the covers of their books or taken by surprise by, in fact, how much they like them. I feel as if I've been lucky from the start in having at least some part in each cover that was used. Let me mention only two of my book covers, the first, *Hush*, and the most recent, my twelfth collection, *Prayer for My Daughter*.

My first full book of poems, *Hush*, was accepted by Jon Galassi, who'd just taken over the newly-revived *Houghton Mifflin New Poetry Series*. Jon was quick to tell me that the cover format for the series was to have a picture of the poet on the cover—not just "on" the cover, but as the full cover.

In 1975, I'd just moved to Oberlin to begin teaching and I didn't know anyone who might take a photograph that might be usable. Then, I discovered that one of my fiction writing students, Peter Ruchman—clearly older by several years, wiser, hipper and more experienced than any of the others in his cohort—had for a while worked in New York as the assistant to the portrait photographer, Arnold Newman. I asked Peter if he was up for this book cover gig and he just laughed, saying, *Sure*, so we set a midday time the next Saturday for him to come by my barely moved-into place.

I was living in an apartment at the edge of Oberlin that had come totally unfurnished. Two of my colleagues who were married and upgrading their home furniture generously gave me a wonderful old settee they'd been storing, adding to it a small round wood table with two wooden chairs. Except for a mattress I'd tossed into the one bedroom, that settee, table and chairs were the only furniture in that apartment.

When Peter arrived with his very beautiful, professional camera, I knew I was in good hands. I saw that he had an open shoebox with twenty-four rolls of thirty-six exposure black-and-white film. Peter had also brought a case of beer that he put down on the small round wood table. Twenty-four rolls of film and twenty-four cans of Pabst Blue Ribbon. Peter was clearly a professional. He was also a brilliant storyteller and for almost an hour we just laughed and swapped stories and drank beer. I could see him watching me through his tinted glasses as we talked and finally realized he wanted me to be, well, extremely relaxed but not yet actually drunk. He gave me a nod and I stood up, sort of, a little wobbly and put on my one sport coat, a brown corduroy all-purpose disguise I could pull out for any emergency. I was also wearing one of the plain sweater-vests I wore in the mid-70s because I was a guy from California who was always cold in Iowa and Ohio.

I managed the dozen steps from the table to the settee and sat back. Peter, standing, began moving to different angles, taking shots continuously as we kept on telling stories. He'd ask me to move slightly or change positions slightly, all the while periodically removing the used rolls and quickly loading new rolls of film. There was an incredible grace and ease as he moved and the action was simply part of the continuum of his shifts of focus. After almost an hour, he nodded and said, *Ok, I know we've got something good here.*

A few days later, Peter came back with the proof sheets. I was amazed to see that, in the photographs Peter had taken, I was able to recognize myself as myself. I looked relaxed (no surprise) but present. The worn settee looked elegant, and no one could ever have guessed it was a lonely settee in that bare room. In the bottom right-hand corner of the photograph, the one we'd selected to send on to Houghton Mifflin, sat (half in view) a single Pabst Blue Ribbon can. It's now forty-eight years since *Hush* was first published, yet I still have people coming up after a reading to praise the totemic presence of that Pabst can.

·

From June 2023 through July, 2024, I lived in Richmond, Virginia; for most of that time I lived in a stone cottage just below a bend of the James

River. Most of my books were in storage, but I had facsimile copies of three of Yeats' most famous books: *The Wild Swans at Coole*, *The Tower*, and *The Winding Stair*. At nineteen, at Fresno State College, in my poetry classes with Philip Levine and my British Lit classes with a wonderful professor, Stanley Poss, I'd spent the year immersed in Yeats work. Four years later, a graduate class with Gayatri Spivak on Baudelaire, Yeats, Mallarmé and Rilke engraved in me a life long connection of those poets.

The covers of those three Yeats books were all designed by his friend, the poet, writer and artist, Sturge Moore, who was a superb wood engraver. Moore's cover designs for Yeats' books remain, for me, some of the most moving and powerful I've ever seen.

In February of 2024, I had a conversation with a longtime friend, scholar and professor Theresia de Vroom, publisher of the new, independent Walton Well Press, based in Los Angeles and Oxford. We discussed the possibility of me joining the press before their October 2024 press launch. I'd just revised, for its final time, a new manuscript of poems, *Prayer For My Daughter*. The title poem, of course, echoes Yeats' famous poem of the same title. Theresia asked if there was anything that I might like if I joined her new press. I said, "I've always wanted a book that looks a hundred years old. I'd love to have a book that looks like one of Sturge Moore's designs for Yeats." Later that day, Theresia texted to say she had an early edition copy of *The Wild Swans* at Coole on its way to her and that her designer, Ash Good, would be able to use this at the basis for the cover of *Prayer For My Daughter*.

It is impossible to describe how appropriate and intimate this cover is; I could never have imagined a striking book. A friend noted the way, in Sturge Moore's design, a parent swan seems to be hovering above and guarding over a younger swan below, in flight. The poem, *Prayer for My Daughter*, is the poem closest to me of all my poems. The book is filled with elegies and departures, losses and reflections, passages of illness. The union of this book and its cover has become, to me, the folding of one long-held dream upon another.

Ellen Bass

Some Thoughts on Juxtaposition in Poetry

LIKE AN ARTIST ASSEMBLING a collage or a film editor splicing scenes, poets build tension, friction, surprise and meaning through juxtaposition. By putting things side-by-side without explanation, we invite the reader into the poem to consider the relationship. This can create a sense of paradox, incongruity, fragmentation, disjunction, tension, or epiphany. In addition to being flexible in the effect it creates; juxtaposition is also flexible in its form. It can operate at the level of diction, syntax, detail, image, rhythm, shape, and idea. Juxtaposition is a strategy that invites readers to engage, to participate in the poem. And juxtaposition reflects the push and pull, the complexity of our actual lives.

I've always loved what Pablo Picasso said:

> "What a sad fate for a painter who loves blondes, but who refrains from putting them in his picture because they don't go with the basket of fruit! What misery for a painter who hates apples to be obliged to use them all the time because they go with the cloth! I put everything I love in my pictures. So much the worse for the things, they have only to arrange themselves with one another."[1]

And a thought from Jane Hirshfield from her book *Ten Windows*:

> "Cognitive and creative discoveries are made in much the same way as much of biological life is: by acts of generative recombination. Disparate elements are brought together to see if they might make a viable new whole . . . Creative epiphany is much the same: a knowledge won against the patterns of predictable thought, feeling, or phrase.
>
> "Surprise, then, is epiphany's first flavor. It is the emotion by which we register shifted knowledge, in a poem, in a life."[2]

I'm going to turn now to a poem of mine, so that I can give an example of the genesis of a poem that relies heavily on juxtaposition. We know that it's not enough to tell "what happened." We have to find the poem in the experience. Sometimes that takes me years of failed attempts, but in this case the muse had mercy and it only took a few months.

Laundry

The baby's dragged the sheets to the kitchen
and now she's stuffing them in the washer,
one hand lifting a wad of yellow cotton,
the other reaching down for more and more. Breathing heavy,
she's feeding vast swathes by the armful,
bent halfway into the mouth of the machine,
a strip of skin exposed where her shirt's ridden up,
an edge of diaper sticking out of her pants.
Who can watch a child and not feel fear
like static in the background or a tinnitus you try to ignore.
This morning in the *Times*, I saw the galaxy LEDA 2046648—
each spiral arm distinct and bright against the dark ink. Light
from a billion years ago, just as the first
multicellular life emerged on Earth.
What are the not-quite-two-years of this intent creature
in the sweep of time? Her quadriceps and scapula,
the alveoli of her lungs, twenty-seven bones of her hand
that evolved from the fin of an ancient fish.
And her scribbly hair sticking up from her first pony tail.
When she was in her mother's body,
the California fires turned the air a smoky topaz
and the sun glowed orange on the kitchen wall.
Last month the floodwaters rose and seeped under the door.
But still, there must be time for this, to watch her—
hands deep into the doing, she's wedded
to the things of this world.
When she stands, her sleeve slips down
and she pushes it up like any woman at work.

—Ellen Bass
from *The New Yorker* (May, 2024)

Okay, let's take it from the top and look at the way juxtaposition works here. And afterward I'll share some of the process of writing the poem:

Laundry

So this opening section is all description of the action of the baby. Eight lines of description in two long sentences. The power of this poem is in the action and that's firmly established before we move on to other thoughts.

The baby's dragged the sheets to the kitchen
and now she's stuffing them in the washer,
one hand lifting a wad of yellow cotton,
the other reaching down for more and more. Breathing heavy,
she's feeding vast swathes by the armful,
bent halfway into the mouth of the machine,
a strip of skin exposed where her shirt's ridden up,
an edge of diaper sticking out of her pants.

And then we make a leap from the scene in the kitchen with the laundry to the speaker's feelings about this scene:

Who can watch a child and not feel fear
like static in the background or a tinnitus you try to ignore.

Now we have the juxtapositions of love and fear and of knowledge and innocence. And the beginning of the juxtaposition of woman and baby, which in the final image of the poem, is going to merge when the baby pushes up her sleeve like any woman at work.

This background static is the underlying, omnipresent awareness of environmental collapse *and* the general background noise in the world and in our minds, *and also* the background static from the Big Bang, the cosmic microwave background radiation.

So when we take the next leap to the LEDA galaxy, there's been a subtle foreshadowing of the cosmic realm.

Next we go back in time just a few hours to the morning paper, and that also takes us back a billion years ago. One of the juxtapositions in this poem is in the realm of time.

This morning in the *Times*, I saw the galaxy LEDA 2046648—
each spiral arm distinct and bright against the dark ink. Light

from a billion years ago, just as the first
multicellular life emerged on Earth.

So we have a galaxy juxtaposed with a kitchen. And then this question that juxtaposes the baby's not-quite two years with a billion years.

What are the not-quite-two years of this intent creature
in the sweep of time?

Now we go into the body of the child. We were just in the body of the galaxy and then the first multicellular bodies and out of all that evolution comes the body of the child.

Her quadriceps and scapula,
the alveoli of her lungs, twenty-seven bones of her hand
that evolved from the fin of an ancient fish.

So we keep juxtaposing: the hand of the child/the fin of the fish.

And her scribbly hair sticking up from her first pony tail.

The poem is also juxtaposing diction here. Scientific language of LEDA 2046648, multicellular life, scapula and alveoli all juxtaposed with "her scribbly hair sticking up from her first pony tail."

Then we leap back into the more recent past (more recent than a billion years ago) to before the baby was born, and we move into the particular reason for the fear: the climate crisis and, specifically, the way it's impacted this family personally. When we're talking about big concerns, it's usually important that we find some way to move from the generic, the abstract, to something specific enough that we can feel it.

When she was in her mother's body,
the California fires turned the air a smoky topaz
and the sun glowed orange on the kitchen wall.
Last month the floodwaters rose and seeped under the door.

And then, juxtaposed with the fear, a refusal to miss out on the present.

But still, there must be time for this, to watch her—
hands deep into the doing, she's wedded
to the things of this world.
When she stands, her sleeve slips down
and she pushes it up like any woman at work.

I'll just mention that this is a poem that ends on an image. It's conclusion is "But still, there must be time for this," but ending with that statement would close the poem down more tightly. Instead, it makes that statement and then reflects on it and describes the child again—the action of the child—pushing up her sleeve and ends with "like any woman at work." The child is joined to all the women of the world. She's going to take her place in the world. And there's going to be plenty of work to do. Although we don't know how she will face this challenge when she's an adult, for now, at least, she pushes up her sleeve and gets down to work. So there's an implicit hope that she has the strength and will to keep at the work of the world.

I want to talk a little about the making of this poem just to give you a sense of how one person—me—worked to create juxtaposition. I have about fifteen drafts of this poem, but I'm only including a couple, which I hope will give a pretty good idea of the progression.

Here's the first one, started February 14, 2023. I started with pieces. I didn't know how they would fit together, but I had two basic pieces to begin with: the action of the baby loading the washer and the image of the LEDA galaxy that I'd read about in the *Times*. You might start a poem with more pieces than this, but even two give you a way to avoid staying on the same note. As Richard Hugo says in his famous book, *The Triggering Town*:

> "There are a few people who become more interesting the longer they stay on a single subject. But most people are like me, I find. The longer they talk about one subject, the duller they get."[3]

It may be tedious to read this first version word for word, so you can just glance over it. But I include it to show how messy a first draft can be and also because there's a phrase I want to call attention to:

> **First Draft of the poem that became "Laundry"**
> February 14, 2023
>
> One by one, the baby's dragged the sheets to the kitchen,
> and now she's stuffing them in the washer, one hand
> lifting a big wad of yellow cotton, the other reaching
> down for more and more. She's feeding the vast swathes
> by the armful, piling it up like the drapery in some lesser
> Rubens or Carravagio, an exuberance of superfluous
> abundance. She's bent over, diaper sticking up, breathing heavy.

Her knees are bent. She's wearing a shirt with woodland
animals playing on it, but she's not playing.

The pattern on the child's shirt isn't, ultimately, important in the poem, but in my first drafts, I try to keep all the doors and windows open for anything to enter, and it turns out that by describing the child's shirt, I get to the woodland animals playing, which leads me to say the child's *not* playing—that this is actual work she's doing—which leads to the last word of the poem! That's why we say that it's in the act of writing that you discover the poem.

When the sleeve
slips down over her hand, she pushes it up and keeps on
I'm told that a baby at two is, pound for pound,
the strongest she'll ever be. She's doing the work
of learning to be a human in this family in California in 2023
when we still have washers and water gushes into machines.
Who can watch a child and not feel dread?

With every great handful she gathers, the cloth drapes and folds,
the light catching it, the dark folds, the yellow is golden,

her hair is a sticking up like a pony tail, but the elastic is gone

when she leans over there's

only at the end when she goes to close the door does she look up with a smile of accomplishment pants

with the effort and with the excitement
there's so much of it

when her shirt lifts up, there's a band of bare skin and the diaper sticks out of her pants

I could tell you how anyone who loves a child always has dread in the background, static in the background

today I won't think about her future and all that could befall her that dread that slashes the night like a siren, red

No, there has to be time just to watch her little arms pull that great wad of gold, her breath panting, her stuffed up nose, she's beyond joy, beyond fun, she's deep into something we could call doing, the doing-ness, the joy of making, satisfaction, accomplishment.

She lifts her arm and shakes her sleeve down, this is the artist at work,
 the
This morning in the times, the LEDA galaxy was a brightness
against the dark ink, light that shone from it a billion
years ago. When the early multicellular organisms emerged on Earth.
What are the two years of this one creature in the swath of that?
It slashes the night.

She's wedded to the things of this world

You can see that much of what the poem needs is already there in the first draft. Unfortunately, that's not always the case with my poems, but obviously, it's a big help when it is.

With this poem, I then made quite a few more drafts. I won't drag you through them all. But in the next draft I'm including you can see there's more coherence even visually. It's no longer in tatters. The galaxy LEDA is woven into the poem now, for example. And evolution, specifically the evolution of her body, is introduced, as well as the specifics about the local wildfires and floods that takes the generic dread to specific causes and the way this speaker and the baby, have experienced it firsthand.

Another Draft of the poem that became "Laundry"

The baby dragged the sheets to the kitchen, one by one,
and now she's stuffing them in the washer,
one hand lifting a wad of yellow cotton, the other reaching down
for more and more. She's feeding vast swathes
by the armful, gathering it up like the drapery in some lesser
Rubens or Caravaggio. An exuberance of superfluous abundance.
Breathing heavy,
she's bent halfway into the mouth of the washer,
a strip of caramel skin exposed where her shirt's ridden up,
an edge of diaper sticking out of her pants.
It's Santa Cruz circa 2023 when we still have water
gushing into machines. Who can watch a child and not feel fear
like static in the background, like a tinnitus you try to ignore.
This morning in the *Times*, I saw the galaxy LEDA 2046648—

each spiral arm distinct and bright against the dark ink. Light
from a billion years ago, just as the first
multicellular life emerged on Earth.
What are the not-quite-two-years of this intent creature
in the sweep of time? Her quadriceps and scapula,
the alveoli of her lungs, the 27 bones of her hand
that evolved from the fin of an ancient fish.
And her scribbly hair sticking up from her first pony tail.
When she was in her mother's body,
the California fires turned the air a smoky topaz
and the sun glowed orange on the kitchen wall.
Last month the floodwaters rose.
But still, there must be time for this, to watch her
as she pulls and pushes the gleaming expanse of the material world.
And as a poet once wrote, the yes is taking over.
Hands deep into the doing, she's wedded
to the things of this world.
When she stands, her sleeve slips down
and she pushes it back up like any woman at work.

I want to mention the Rubens or Caravaggio lines which leave the poem in the final draft. I spent a good few hours looking at their paintings and I loved the sound of them, but when I showed this draft to my friend, the brilliant poet, Frank X Gaspar, he said, *Language I think moves attention away from the baby*... I'm just taken with the focus on the baby's action and how it makes the poem live. The skin, the shirt, the diaper sticking out of her pants . . . I see her so viscerally." Immediately, I knew he was right. Detail has to be both vivid and essential and this was not only not essential, as Frank said, it moved the attention away from what was.

My hope is that walking through the way this poem uses juxtaposition might be encouraging and also instructive—to see how it's possible to start with a first draft that has a lot of what it needs, but is still pretty ragged, and then begin to give it shape, to add more in, to take some out, and then consider chronology, essential versus non-essential detail, sound, music, and all the other elements of the craft.

In closing, a final thought from the critic Robert Shattuck:

> "Juxtaposition, with its surprises and intimacy of form, brings the spectator closer than ever before to the abruptness of creative process . . ."[4]

1 Pablo Picasso, quoted by Richard Friedenthal in *Letters of the Great Artists—from Blake to Pollock* (Thames & Hudson, 1963)

2 Jane Hirshfield, "Poetry and the Constellation of Surprise," from *Ten Windows: How Great Poems Transform the World* (Knopf, 2015)

3 Richard Hugo, *The Triggering Town: Lectures and Essays on Poetry and Writing* (W. W. Norton & Company, 1979)

4 Robert Shattuck, quoted in Tony Hoagland, "Fragment, Juxtaposition, and Completeness," *Real Sofistikashun* (Graywolf Press, 2006)

Amber Flora Thomas

A Journey Between Poetry & Art

THE FIRST TIME I TRANSFORMED a memory into sensual description, I fell in love with poetry. I finished the tight narrative arc with an epiphany—that concise rendering of a truth both simple and profound that surprised even me. In the poem, I handed the body of a slaughter animal to the woman of the house and felt resolution, in the confines of a neatly lined page, for an experience that had haunted me for years. It seemed finished, strained from my body and my mind, and so laden with detail that I was sure a reader might flinch at the touch of a pinky. I offered it to my workshop group a few days later. Here, I thought, now you, dear readers, can revel in the pain I've lived with my entire life.

Until this moment, bent over the page in my single bed at the start of my second year of college, I had not known what to do with my ugly past, but this, this was the shape of things to come. In the safety of my new life, hundreds of miles from the circumstances and people who had crippled me emotionally, I could image-out a usable story and truth. With the certainty of all teenagers, I believed wholly that an image could transform anything. Here was some darkness spun with wing and leg; it was as fine as a knife when I handled it in a poem.

Yet, I had been living in the figurative since my eyes had first learned to focus. Floors cluttered with Dad's wire woven sculptures of larger-than-life disembodied man heads. I thought of them as brainy escapades with their circuity exposed. The copper and brass wire that spiraled, feeding mouths knotted closed, eyes flat with red jasper pupil. They were in a god-voice that offered no words and gazed up distressingly at their creator, my father.

Gazing up to any windowsill, wall, or shelf I'd find the pouring notes of purples, blues, and greens in my mother's abstract watercolors and acrylic paintings. I'd swim in her impressionistic vision where exaggerated light and shadow made the landscape moodier. She took liberties with colors, so I'd never seen such a blush or burnishing of emerald anywhere else.

In between reading the *I Ching* and Bhagavata had my father secretly been studying the human nervous system? Did my mother need a pair of glasses? When I asked them the story behind these creations, they mentioned needing to make a buck. We needed to survive somehow because neither of my parents worked. They tended to their art.

Guitars leaning in a corner, artwork cluttering every room, they wrote songs and poetry, as well. Late at night they worked out the cords to folksy ballads that I grew to hate after hearing them hundreds of times. We were often hungry, we were often in despair about where to live, or how to pay for food and gas. Dad would get drunk, and his laughter would turn into rage which turned into sobbing tears. Both smoked pot upon waking, and throughout the day. Image: a joint stuck between his lips, Dad smiling at me as he bent a long length of copper wire into a spiral. Image: Mom tipping the ash off a joint at the kitchen sink. They were remaking the world as they saw it. Their middle class straightlaced upbringings abandoned for art.

I grew up on art shows, flea markets, and street bazaars. In the 1970s, you could meet my parents at Venice Beach in Los Angeles, wire woven jewelry spread on a table, guitars out, a couple bucks and some coins started in the hat between their feet. "Dance," Dad would yell at my siblings and I. "Dance," which we did until we realized that no one else was dancing, crowds of beach goers pushing past our pitiful ensemble.

Without knowing it, how I saw the world was being complicated by their artistic visions. The words that come to mind are dispersal, chaos, indecision. "Nothing keeps my eye still in there," I wrote in "Eye of Water" as I tried to describe my mother's paintings. In "Conversation with the Sculptor," I described my father's efforts as making bodies "out of knots." And so often when I've written about my father, something is woven or wrapping itself in his presence.

When I finally started writing the poems that would make up my first book, I discovered that fractures, or fragments, both of memory and image, were enough to hold up the entirety of my sight. "I want to be the wrecker of this," I wrote in response to a memory of the early morning pristine mirror of Young Lakes in Yosemite, as I found myself wishing to "glide / toward a danger of no geography" ("Water Answering Sky and Mountain"). That I've found myself living all over the United States is perhaps a sign of how prophetic poetry can be at times. I was always going to be the kind of poet who "gets into puddles with the sky" because nothing had been in proportion to sense for most of my life ("Damaged Photos").

For a long time, I felt bitter about how often we found ourselves starving or destitute in broken-down vehicles on the side of the road when I was a child, but what a gift to have parents consumed by the need for something more than just survival. Soon after I moved to North Carolina for my second tenure-track teaching position at a small university, I started my own art business. Saturdays, I get up around 4:15 AM to drive to an outdoor market a few towns away. After I have my art pieces hung and displayed, I prop my poetry books in the middle of the table, and it seems the story of my own artistic pursuit is complete, although still perplexing to me.

While I have not been destitute since I was a student, I was compelled to start the business so I could save money for a downpayment on my house. Last year, I built a studio in the back yard to extricate the clutter of ongoing projects which had taken over every surface and corner inside my house.

On a perfect day, I move between the page and my crafting table. I like to work with broken things, the strong remnants of what is left when something dies. Like driftwood, which is the strongest part of a tree that has endured seasons of ocean and river currents to be worn into shapes that sometimes appear as animals. Or the sea glass I collected during my youth in Mendocino, California, a remnant representing our long history of dumping trash right into the sea and those forces finding the strongest core to mold into a gleaming gem. Abalone shell is perhaps my favorite material, which I also gather in Mendocino when I visit friends and family. My brother has been helpful in shipping what he can find once or twice a year, as well.

My passion for thrift stores has added to my arsenal of materials as I find antique and vintage dishware, single cups and pitches long detached from their wedding sets, which I turn into planters and birdfeeders. Sometimes I break cracked or damaged glass bowls and vases further to tumble the shards and make strikingly new sea glass-like pieces. The remnants of lives, the evidence of a life before. These land on my craft table and become a new story as wind chime, wall art, sun catcher, jewelry even.

The natural composition of everything is to be part and parcel of something else. I didn't have to work very hard to find this conversation within my artwork. I am always thinking about narrative and how to show a larger story through fragments of memory, as well as what washes up on shore. I find myself obsessed with line, the falling vertical curve, the climbing horizontal reach, the round meeting the sharp. When I suspend crystals and bells from a driftwood branch, wow, a piece that will speak to the sun and the wind, bringing nature a bit closer to the person who hangs this work in a window or on a porch. And don't we all need to be a bit closer to nature these days?

Sometimes a customer will buy a copy of one of my books and one of my artistic creations, and I feel . . . yes! Yes, I can do it all, be a writer and an artist. That what has grown out of my work as a poet is this natural evolution—the arc, the narrative, which I think I can speak about succinctly in a few different forms. There is joy in a life-long endeavor to heal and be healed through the forms that art offers.

Spencer Rumsey

No Spontaneous Bop Prosody!

A Professional Editor's Advice to Poets Writing Prose

THE OTHER DAY in my journal, I found a cartoon I'd saved about the editing profession. An aspiring young writer faces a no-nonsense professional who explains that his literary opus plopped on the desk between them does indeed have commercial potential. As she tells him: "With ruthless editing and extensive rewrites, this could be the next lackluster American Novel."

In my checkered career as an editor, I didn't worry about the best-seller lists. I didn't edit literary fiction, but I did work with a vast array of authors, from Pulitzer Prize-winning columnists to unabashed amateurs who had a good story to tell, as long as their words didn't get in the way. My role was to help writers reach more readers by conveying their truth as compellingly as possible, without missing a deadline or overlooking an egregious error.

My first full-time editing job came at the *Berkeley Barb*, once one of the largest underground papers in California. But at the end of the Seventies, the unpopular Vietnam War had ended, and this plucky weekly paper was on its last legs. In theory, we were still a band of Fourth Estate radicals open to everything, especially if it meant shocking the bourgeoisie. There I learned how much experience matters. First-time authors might fight me tooth and nail as I tried to revise their precious revolutionary prose because they'd convinced themselves that their words were carved in stone—even if they'd written their story while they were stoned. Fortunately for me, writers who'd been published before were much more congenial to work with, because I'd make it clear from the beginning that it would always be their byline, not mine, on their finished work.

Some Do's and Don'ts for Submitting & Writing Non-fiction Prose

Every Monday morning when I reported for duty at Rupert Murdoch's supermarket tabloid *Star Magazine*, where I quickly had to memorize Elizabeth Taylor's marriages in chronological order, the first thing we "rim rats" on the copy desk would ask our copy chief was this million-dollar question: "Any libel or lawsuits?" Invariably he'd shake his head, and proudly confirm, "Not today!" We knew what we were hired to do—and how far we dared to go. I lasted there almost four years.

Boredom is always the enemy, especially in nonfiction because you don't want the facts to bog the story down. Once a talented *Star* reporter turned in her first draft with this opening line: "I spent the night in a haunted house and nothing happened!" Her exclamation mark wasn't enough. We had to redo the lede just to trick readers into entering the story.

I regard editing as a balancing act. Of course, you want to liberate every sentence from jargon, rhetoric and clichés. Although as an old tabloid editor, I've always had a soft spot for bad puns, but in good measure. Once at *Star*, an aspiring writer submitted a story that he tried to juice up by describing the locale as having "trout-infested waters." That went over the line, so I cut it.

Years later as an op-ed editor at *New York Newsday* and *Newsday*, I had the time to ensure that the contributing writers were on board with every revision. If our interaction proved fruitful, our editorial banter might produce better points that hadn't been considered—or had been discarded by the author in their deadline rush.

And that point is worth reiterating, especially in the digital age. Back in the day, I'd tell myself that my copyediting was nearly perfect until I spoke it out loud. Hearing those words would raise issues, whether large or small, factual or structural, especially about the flow of the prose—or as poets might say, when it's time to breathe.

The devil's in the details. For a brief news item, everything that's important for the reader to know has to appear right up front. Longer pieces can take their time getting their points across. Yet sometimes, the most engaging element that could make the reporting unique might get cut arbitrarily. This is where the writer's viewpoint is key. At *Newsday,* my friend wrote a story about an elderly suburban man found dead in his living room easy chair. His body had been decomposing there a year. It was only discovered when a utility worker came to investigate why the electric bill hadn't been paid. The TV had never been turned off. The copyeditor had wanted to cut that fact, but she insisted it remain in the lede. She was right. In print, it caught the attention of late-night TV hosts who spread that sadly mundane story to millions of people far beyond *Newsday*'s circulation.

As a Sixties kid, I grew to appreciate Jack Kerouac's "spontaneous bop prosody." Later, in my career, I wondered how an editor would handle Kerouac's breakthrough style, since I knew how much he valued his "first thought, best thought" mantra. Luckily for me, I had the chance to ask his agent, Sterling Lord, at a Kerouac commemorative event in Northport, where he'd lived with his mom. Lord told me that a wonderful copyeditor—he didn't say who—was the unsung hero for *On the Road,* the novel that put the "king of the beats" on the map. The editor was also a musician, so she respected the rhythms of his prose. But Kerouac resented any interference, no matter how sympathetic. After that book became a bestseller in 1957, Lord helped his successful client gain total control of his every word subsequently. That's what his author wanted, Lord told me with a shrug, but none of his other books ever did as well.

The moral of this story is that even a great writer can benefit from good editing.

Eileen R. Tabios

(Title Below)

IN THE GARDEN, the oleander shrub was massive, about 18 feet high and 24 feet wide. I usually ignored its greenery as backdrop for much of the year, but in the summer, it grabbed any backyard visitor's attention since it had sprouted, as I wrote in the poem about it,

> braggadocious clusters of blooms
> radiating whites, pinks and reds
> easily holding up the non-fallen sky

Four stanzas later, however, the poem switched gears to refer to a murder in the Philippines that I'd just learned the prior night:

> Stunned, I learned even the smallest fragment
> from your thin petals can send my dogs
> to join you, Kerima Lorena Tariman
>
> killed by the Armed Forces' 70th Infantry
> Battalion in Silay City, Negros Occidental
> on August 20, 2021—the evening before
>
> the 38th anniversary of the assassination
> of Benigno Aquino, Jr., sparking other People's
> Revolutions around the world . . .

I did not expect that my poem, inspired by the magnificently sprouting *Nerium Oleander*, would lead to the murder of 42-year-old activist and poet Tariman, who was wounded in a battle between the New People's Army and the Philippine military in Negros Occidental, Philippines. The former managing editor of the University of the Philippines' *Philippine Collegian*, Tariman and her husband, poet-musician Ericson Acosta (who was killed about three months later in similar circumstances), had left their son behind in Manila to live in Negros where they fought for the poor and landless. Negros has long suffered from a sugar hacienda lifestyle as well as polluted mining; the province once received global attention for a 78% infant malnourishment rate during the 1970s/80s. In fact, as an undergraduate student at Barnard College, I wrote a political science paper on the conflict of interests between politicians charged with guiding the country's development on behalf of the entire population, while belonging to wealthy families whose status quo they were incentivized to preserve if not enhance: the gap between rich and poor has widened. My poem ends with the hope:

> Kerima's flower shall be generous with seeds
> blossoming to grow a Homeland no longer
> Imaginary, no longer abstracted by corruption
> We are a people as hardy as you and, soon
> our Motherland shall be watered by other
> sources than the veins of sacrificed poets.

I am glad my poem ended remembering Kerima Lorena Tariman. But I did not plan or anticipate the result, though I can understand how a mention of killing or its possibility—for example, by the oleander's poisonous petals—and as enhanced by my decades-long awareness of Negros' plight might evoke the revolutionary working and dying in the province known as the "Sugarbowl of the Philippines."

But I'm not surprised my would-be flower poem traveled elsewhere and far. As I consider this effect, I recall a book by Maureen Owen, *Zombie Notes* (Sun Books, 1985), where titles don't always remain atop poems. In another book, *The No-Travels Journal,* the title of her poem, "Paris Blues," is placed at the bottom of the verse. That format exemplifies how my better poems work: I don't know their titles until I've completed writing them (or their first drafts). My poem ended up being entitled "*Nerium Oleander,* Shorter Than Kerima." I certainly could not conceive of that title before finishing the poem, which appears in my new Marsh Hawk book *Because I Love You, I Become War.*

The poems, themselves, will provide their titles. It seems so basic to me now, but not if one understands that I'm like many who've been taught or introduced to poems as something that's *about* something. But to approach a poem's creation that way is, for me, too paradigmatic or stifling. The poem often transcends authorial intent and must be free to go where it chooses.

I've learned that my role as a poet is to capture a burst of something—whether it's a feeling or a resonant single word or an image (like the gloriously flowering oleander)—that would open the door to the rest of the poem. My poems *become* due to their writing process, e.g., a word surfaces only because of the prior word or phrases. There's a saying, "Poems write themselves," and such has been my experience.

As a result, much of my job as a poet takes place before I begin any poem. My job is to educate myself on as many topics as possible, engage in a wide variety of experiences, hone my skills at observation, and meditate over the significance of a variety of events—not for writing a poem but by being better in the world through a basking in experience. All this knowledge and experience are filed in my brain as raw material for when I finally write the poem, e.g., the information on Negros Occidental which had marinated in my mind for three decades. In the actual creation of the poem, I trust in having filed enough mental material for the poem to access as it chooses.

Obviously, the more content there is in that mental file, the better the poem is served. I recently noted in an interview that as a poet I believe in education for education's sake for avoiding cliches and sourcing new metaphors. As an example, for no particular reason besides education, I learned about black holes, specifically, that if one is able to witness the phenomenon, one would see objects falling into those holes in falls that seem never to end. The idea of a *permanent falling* resonated with me and came to be included in several poems.

It is only after the poem informs me of its last word, that I then can discover its title. For a similar example, I didn't know what this essay's title would be until I wrote it. Here's the title:

Freeing the Poem from the Poet

Stephen Paul Miller

The Poetry Mailing List: Poetry Beyond Borders

"1976"

After his reading I asked Peter Schjeldahl for a
poem
for our one-page magazine folded in an envelope.

"I haven't written a poem in two years. You don't know?"

Later that night Peter found himself talking to "Verse"
as if thinking over my plan to bypass everything but poetry through
new Xerox
technology.

"Your business is pleasure,"
Peter found himself telling
"the Art of Verse"
in the poem
he mailed me early the next morning.

That afternoon, I mailed the world two
or three hundred copies—the world was smaller then—folding,
addressing,
stuffing, stamping, and sealing "Dear Art of Verse" exactly

as he typed it. The next day one person after another called

him, each thinking he sent the poem
only to them. Amazed
he asked me over,
showed up at my art show,
and *The Poetry Mailing List*
still thrills him, a little

before he announced
he had

terminal cancer.
I feel he's okay.

Time can't be real.

September 22, 2022

In April 1977, I wander into the Andy Warhol Factory building's elevator.

I get off at maybe the third floor and there's Andy. I saw him before, in Heiner Friedrich's Wooster Street gallery, where Warhol projected a shrewd art-world-guy aura wearing perfectly fitting blue jeans with a beautiful black belt, but now he pumps out his coolly enthusiastic big-baby character. I show him my one-page poetry magazine, *The Poetry Mailing List,* and boy, did he love it! My single-poet journal makes his eyes pop.

After all, in the mid-seventies, clean cheap Xeroxing was new. I saw it as a vehicle for making something that was nothing but poetry. I conceived a total focus on poetry. I thought Jasper Johns had done something like that with painting. With *Flag* (1954-1955) he eliminated the abstraction of both explicit and implied representation by making his painting nothing but a sign. This paradoxically freed him to make his painting nothing but painting by jettisoning any hint of copying nature.

I similarly wanted to eliminate all the distraction surrounding poetry and bypass the sentinels of publication by simply mailing poetry. I thought of all poetry, however, as visual and verbal hybrids. Sometimes, in the *PML,* poems were part of an art piece, but even when they were not, I thought of them as visual art in three ways. First, if there were no accompanying images, I thought of the poem as presenting an implicitly iconoclastic reality. Second, every issue was contextualized by a small *PML* logo and issue number. Third, since this was well before personal computers, a poet's individual way of typing and/or writing seemed beautifully authentic. John Cage, for example, made a point of wanting to know exactly how to type his mesostic poem:

John Cage's Special Offer

"Would you like a drink?"

the great 20th century
master John Cage asked.

“Very much,” I overstated,
amazed to be sitting
in his basement studio.

After his Town Hall concert,
I asked Cage for a short poem
for my one-page poetry journal.

“Call me,” said Cage.
When I phoned, he asked,
“Can you come get it now?”

Knowing I would Xerox cheap,
clean copies,
then a revelation—

he asked how
I wanted his poem on the page.
I stood above him

as he typed.
His large flush left margin
thrilled both of us.

Afterward he asked,
“Would you like my special tea?”
“Yes.”

He floated to his kitchen area
to bring me a tall thin cylindrical
mug without a handle

though I liked
strong, sweet Indian
chai with a kick,

Cage’s tea
was the opposite
and that was the point.

"It levels you. Some people,"
he continued,
"like caffeine. They like the bump

it gives you." Cage paused
and said,
"I don't like that bump."

"Sometimes I like the bump,"
I told him, "but I love your tea's flat,
bitter aftertaste."

Cage beamed and said,
My new diet is wonderful.
I'm feeling better all the time.
When I die
I'll be in perfect health."

In addition to Cage, David Shapiro, Kathy Acker, Ann Lauterbach, David Lehman, Charles Bernstein, Rudy Burkhardt, Beth Anderson, Michael Goldberg, Robert Ashley, Jonathan Williams, Joel Oppenheimer, Lucio Pozzi, Linda Francis, Peter Schjeldahl, and others contributed. The success of the Poetry Mailing List was guaranteed early on when I ran into John Cage for the first time at Town Hall. When I asked him out of nowhere for a poem, he told me to call him. When I call he tells me to come right over. Appointments are such a drag.

My co-editor, Kenneth Deifik, and I bent our "one-page to maximize focus" ethos and put out multi-page David Shapiro and Kathy Acker issues, in addition to a Jimmy Carter inauguration issue. We got Council for Coordinating Literary Magazine grants. *Poets and Writers* featured a story about *The Poetry Mailing List* by, if memory serves, Nelson Richardson, who interviewed me at the Poets and Writers offices. They published the article with my headshot (see above), which I had made when they asked for a photo. Subscribers sent checks from all over the country. A couple of them said they heard about it on NPR, though I didn't. The new subscribers added to our address base of the Poetry Project mailing list and suggestions in the art and other worlds from sculptor John Newman and others.

As much as I believed in the mechanism of *The Poetry Mailing List,* I also saw it as a way to meet people. I therefore didn't mind it when people I admired didn't contribute their work. Warhol wouldn't contribute but he asked me whom I could interview. "John Ashbery," I said, elating him. Although *Interview* editor Bob Colacello killed the story in favor of a Ricky Ricardo, Jr. and Dino Martin interview, in retrospect, hanging out with John was what mattered.[1]

I can't thank *Chapter One* enough for asking me to write about *The Poetry Mailing List.* If corporations are people, they should all be the *PML.* The process of incorporating as a non-profit organization was exhilarating. The lawyer who contributed his services through the Volunteer Lawyers for the Arts, Felix D'Arienzo, became interested in the poetry he was incorporating. A patent attorney with engineering and law degrees, he was fascinated by my observation that there was poetry in the precision of his technical language designed to prove the unique nature of intellectual property. Out of nowhere, he becomes a lifelong poet. He writes amazing poems in pure patent lawyer language [copyrighting / copywriting] his feelings. As I say introducing him for a June 1978 Ear Inn series reading, "Felix D'Arienzo portends something sturdy and new by simply being himself."

I Google Felix for this article. He's posted new poems! They're a little more sentimental than I remember, but as Delmore Schwartz asked, why should we abhor the sentimental in art but seek it in life? In one poem, Felix stops Time in the street, and Time tells him, 'Within each point of space, there is all time." And he's posted a poem I wrote about him in 1977, "You're Missing Felix"! And my introduction for his reading!

But wait! I'm startled to find out that Felix has recently died.

When I Googled Felix, I thought I had been rude a few years ago when we got together because I forgot to ask how his legal secretary in the seventies, Gerri, was doing. I realize from her post that Felix, or "Fee" as Gerri called him, unexpectedly died. In her short paragraph post, she says, "Felix introduced me to some wonderfully talented artists such as composer Dan Berlinghoff and poet Stephen Paul Miller." That Gerri Czachowski should seemingly so clearly remember me after a brief professional relationship some forty-five years ago blows my mind. I wouldn't trade it for any other professional honor.

Although I no longer run it, The Poetry Mailing List, Inc., as Marsh Hawk Press, Inc., is publishing more poetry than ever; it will outlive me. I see streaks of it in everything I do. In the eighties, for instance, poet

Laurie Perricci desperately asked me where she could be published. I heard John Cage telling me to come right over when I told her to come over with ten or twenty friends. I flashed on a new take on Richard Kostelanetz's *Assembling*, which boxed loose pages of individual contributions, and various Poetry Project magazines that were put together by volunteers at collating events. Why not add a Marxist twist to that kind of assemblage and have the poets do the hard labor of assembling? This would give the workers all the cultural capital. Every month, dozens of poets would come over with their 200 or so copies. Kenneth Deifik came up with the name *The National Poetry Magazine of the Lower East Side.* I sweated such details as a contributor's page, cardboard stock covers, the art on them, and how to bind them. Ron Kolm brought a stapler strong enough to bind all our work, until I bought one. He also brought copies to The St. Mark's Bookstore. Then *The National Poetry Magazine of the Lower East Side* collating moved to bars and restaurants where the collators took turns reading.

It's hard to believe, but as far as I know, that was the first time a regular journal in which so many poets and artists in the process of being published did the assembling. It seems, however, commonplace now.

Coming from one collating party after midnight, I showed the latest issue with a young Meher Baba on the cover to Allen Ginsberg in the Kiev restaurant. He immediately got the Marxist angle. His face lit up. I asked him to write a poem for it on the spot. His friend scoffed at the idea and tried to protect Allen from me, but he told his friend, with whom he seemed to have been editing or doing some other work, to relax.

The notion of doing the "hard work" of *The National Poetry Magazine of the Lower East Side* inspired him. After writing nonstop for a couple of minutes or so, he told me to use the page he gave me however I wanted to send him a copy (which I delivered to him at his weekly Brooklyn College class). Together with "America," "Kaddish," and "White Shroud," it's on my Mount Rushmore of Allen poems:

Hard Work

After midnite, Second Avenue horseradish Beef
at Kiev's wood tables—
The Kasha Mushrooms tastes good
as Byelorussia usta when my momma

ran away from Cossacks 1905
Did the 5 year plan work? How bad Stalin?
Am I a Stalinist? A Capitalist? A
Bourgeois Stinker? A rotten Red?
No I'm a fairy with purple wings and white halo
translucent as an onion ring in
the transsexual fluorescent light of Kiev
Restaurant after a hard day's work

—Allen Ginsberg
February 17, 1986, 12:35 A.M.[2]

At the next monthly collating party, a poet objected to Ginsberg not collating with us. The guy had a point. I should have at least asked Allen to come over.

After a few years, I left America on a Fulbright. When I returned, there were many groups using my Marxist model throughout the country. Most of them never heard of *The National Poetry Magazine of the Lower East Side*. So it goes.

I've always felt bad about dropping the ball on *The Poetry Mailing List*. Doing all that collating, address labeling, folding, and sealing was something I had fun with, but it was nothing to take lightly. A full-time job without any remunerative end in sight, it made graduate school seem practical. On the way to the first day of class, I ran into Kathy Acker, whom I met through the *PML*, in Washington Square Park. She was unreservedly excited for me to be getting a Ph.D. and kept saying how cool it was. Kathy had the sweet superpower of making me never look back. And Kathy was right. School is cool. Every critical idea that got me things like tenure was like the *PML*, in that academicians and professionals didn't get my ideas until they worked. I still don't get the *List*, but I know it's still with me. It's an uncontrollable force, a form of Marxist fun.

When I was a teenager, I was taken by William Blake saying no imaginative act could be lost. I think Walter Benjamin explains why. "Nothing that has ever happened," wrote Benjamin, "should be regarded as lost" because we are the change (however imperfect) the past is banking on. We feel this in our bones, much as we ask the future to redeem us. And yet, past, present, and future redeem one another through "the stand-alone now"—something like what Felix was getting at when he intuited his death.

According to Benjamin, there is no "distinguishing between major and minor events," because we only know them through this independent "now"—*The Poetry Mailing List* of all we know. Every star part of an acausal constellation, everything is poetry without borders.

Somebody might do *The Poetry Mailing List* again, but, even if they don't, my experience with Peter Schjeldahl is a gift that keeps giving. As I tell in this piece's poetic epigraph, the surprise of poetry smacked him in the face. His poem is probably why we called it *The Poetry Mailing List*. It's certainly the name's payoff. The piece he sent me, unavailable anywhere else now, is the best description of the poetic process I've ever read:

Dear Art of Verse

I haven't checked in with you, Verse, in some time.
We've been estranged for about two years,
though I don't flatter myself that you've noticed.
You don't need me to love you, though actually,
to my surprise,
I find I do—having got over for the moment hating you
for not serving me as I once thought you would,
as I pathetically almost felt you ought to.
Your business is pleasure.
My ambition has been—what? Meaning?
Well, I'm still far from cured of that grim yearning
to be useful and clear and well-paid,
but I promise to quit belaboring you with it.
Prose will do for my civil tasks
for which my early devotion to you, Verse, made me limber.
(What was frustrating was finding that your relation to Prose
is a one-way street.)
And so I return to you, sweet science of line-lengths
and line-breaks, laughably called "free,"
though you enslave even your masters, chaste modern instrument
so hard to handle, let alone play—
maybe a half-dozen poets in America right now
seem to know which end to blow into,
and except in two or three self-forgetful flights
I have not been one of them.

You do not lead to will or passion, you are pitiless
in exposing the proud mind, the tendentious heart,
not do you thrill to words like "tendentious"
though you make no fuss, suffering fools in silence.
Your business is pleasure, you are always elsewhere
when anything else is occurring.
When pleasure rules the roost
and the poet observes your strictures,
then the elsewhere is suddenly here
and the heart breaks neatly. And that
is absolutely all there is to it, a simplicity
that has often driven me crazy with rage
and now makes me want to weep with despair.
But only you can make me weep that way, shame me with weeping
as when I can't get through "The Idea of Order at Key West" aloud
without choking, and feeling like an idiot.
The great poems all are based on dumb ideas
to which great minds submit themselves as offerings, burnt
by the blowtorch of pleasure to a fine ash.
You are murder on the nerves, Verse,
with your ecstasies giving a promontory
on the most terrible boredom,
the boredom of the marvelous, unlivable life.
Surely, I think, humans are not born to be so transfixed
by angelic apparitions, by what cannot be gotten,
and then I am tempted to believe with the Marxists
that you yourself, Verse, in your present form,
your office of substitute religion, cannot but be implicated
in our hideously dreary condition, and that History,
the mass human story, is the only ticket
to get us off the dime of a despicable languor, the modern swoon.
(Whether any of this follows only prose can tell.)
But I do not believe that, not here in mid-penance,
for I find that without you I have nothing but anger,
and disdaining you will not keep one person from starving.
Finally your consolation will not be the pleasure
with which you sear us to the core, but the pain that comes after,
the pain of knowing life as a crushing potential.

In this way you gratify life,
which we might otherwise suppose we actually possess
and be doubly fallen. So I'm trying to stop squirming
and to take my joy and terror straight, like a man
who knows what it is to be a poet,
though he may lack endurance for that fierce vocation.

—Peter Schjeldahl
November, 1976

Like Benjamin, Peter sees the need for a different kind of Marxist history. I just think of William Blake, Walter Benjamin, and Peter Schjeldahl. O Boy!

---

1 For more about the interview see: https//blog.bestamericanpoetry.com/ /2017/10/stephen-paul-miller-remembers-john-ashbery-.html *and* https://www.publishersweekly.com/pw/by-topic/columns-and-blogs/soapbox/article/75143-for-poets-there-s-no-such-thing-as-bad-press.html

2 https://dreaminginthedeepsouth.tumblr.com/post/698725171562954752/allen-with-quentin-crisp-at-the-kiev-restaurant

Liane Strauss

How to Help Your Non-Poet Friends Enjoy Poetry More (Maybe)

LOVE THEM, and our digital, "5-minute read" age might seem ideally suited to play matchmaker. But as poets know, poems aren't like data or opinions, which are hard to love for other reasons. Poems are more like people. They require time, effort and attention. Lip-service love isn't enough. Poems like babies may be small, but they make up for it in other ways.

So how do we, poets, help people get what they want when it comes to poetry, and help poems in the process—so we can stop worrying about them?

One possibility is to address common misperceptions.

Poems have a funny reputation. On the one hand, because of nursery rhymes and their presence in so much children's literature, people think of poems as approachable, spontaneous, child's play.

On the other hand, because they seem to belong to the same family as hymns and sermons, and therefore to be associated with matters of the spirit, people think of poems as uplifting. When they are overwhelmed by love or loss, even folks who never normally give poetry a second thought turn to poems for comfort or company.

On the *other* hand, actually sitting down and Reading A Poem™ sounds like work: wading through stilted, archaic, labyrinthine or just plain bewildering phrases while doing a puzzle without knowing the rules—*Doesn't it have to rhyme?*—or if it even has a solution.

On the *other* other hand, there's something about poetry . . .

Maybe the allure has to do with the elusive. Poetry is famously impossible to pin down, though certainly not for lack of trying.[1] Here's just a small, eclectic selection of attempts from a small, eclectic handful of poets:

Samuel Taylor Coleridge: *The best words in the best order.*

Leo Tolstoy: *Everything with the exception of business documents and school books.*

Marianne Moore: *Imaginary gardens with real toads.*

Wallace Stevens: *A revelation of words by means of the words.*

Emily Dickinson: *[What] makes my body so cold no fire ever can warm me.*

Matthew Arnold: *A criticism of life.*

Ezra Pound: *About as much a 'criticism of life' as a red-hot iron is a criticism of fire.*

For me, being a poet means I'm constantly bumping into metaphors, knocking over non-sequiturs and looking under and behind words for the experiences they are valiantly attempting, though often as not failing, to contain. So you'll forgive me when I tell you that all this reminds me of one of my very first trips to the beach.

I was about six, standing by myself just behind the line where the froth of the surf keeps irresistibly melting into the sand. The wind was pounding in my ears, my hair flying every which way, my skin coated in a not altogether unpleasant film of salt and grit. I was watching a boat like an eye on the horizon with some idea that it held the answer to where exactly the far edge of the water met the near edge of the sky when I suddenly found myself on my ass, scrabbling to hold onto ropes of sand that kept tugging me toward the water and disintegrating between my fingers. It was scary and messy and embarrassing—and I kind of hoped it would happen again.

That September, on the first day of first grade, Miss Rimer (yes) sat me next to Alan Wonder (seriously), and it was just like that moment at the beach.

Ever since, if I'm completely exhilarated and spinning out of control, flustered, preoccupied and weirdly serene, walking into lampposts and forgetting to eat, it can only mean one thing. I'm in love.

Or reading a really great poem.

To me, they're two roads to the same happy calamity, metaphors for each other. Once I'd gotten a taste of that feeling of being knocked clear over by some poem—or some one—I wanted more. And that's why, even if the poem I'm reading isn't a love poem, it's always about love.

So when my non-poet friends tell me they can't remember the last time they enjoyed reading a poem, I tell them to take one out for a coffee, or a trip to the beach, and instead of trying to figure it out and pin it down, try just getting to know it—and letting it get to know them—and see what happens next.

There's no guarantee you'll fall in love with poetry, I tell them, *and there's no guarantee you won't.*

---

1 Samuel Johnson, famous for his *Dictionary of the English Language* (1755), cautioned against it: "To circumscribe poetry by a definition will only show the narrowness of the definer." It probably came as no surprise to him that he was spitting in the wind. Under his definition of the word definition: 3. [In logick.] The explication of the essence of a thing by its kind and difference. "What is man? Not a reasonable animal merely; for that is not an adequate and distinguishing *definition. Bentley.*

Author Biographies

Ellen Bass' most recent book is *Indigo* (Copper Canyon, 2020). Her awards include Fellowships from the Guggenheim Foundation, NEA, Lambda Literary Award, and four Pushcart Prizes. She co-edited the first major anthology of women's poetry, *No More Masks!* (Doubleday, 1973), and she co-authored the groundbreaking, *The Courage to Heal: A Guide for Women Survivors of Child Sexual Abuse* (Harper & Row, 1988). Chancellor Emerita of the Academy of American Poets, Bass founded poetry workshops at Salinas Valley State Prison and the Santa Cruz jails. She teaches in Pacific University's MFA program and offers online Living Room Craft Talks at ellenbass.com.

Patricia Carlin has published three books of poetry including, most recently, *Second Nature*. Her work has appeared in numerous journals and anthologies, and she was awarded fellowships from the MacDowell Colony and the Virginia Center for the Creative Arts. She has taught poetry and poetry writing, as well as Shakespeare studies, at Princeton, Vassar and The New School. She co-edits the poetry journal *Barrow Street*.

Denise Duhamel's most recent books of poetry are *Second Story* (Pittsburgh, 2021) and *Scald* (2017). *Blowout* (2013) was a finalist for the National Book Critics Circle Award. She teaches at Florida International University in Miami.

Elaine Equi is the author of many books, including *Ripple Effect: New and Selected Poems* and, most recently, *The Intangibles*. A new collection, *Out of the Blank*, is forthcoming from Coffee House Press. She is also the guest editor of *Best American Poetry 2023*.

Steve Fellner has published two books of poetry from Marsh Hawk Press, *Blind Date with Cavafy* and *The Weary World Rejoices*. In 2021, Ohio State University Press released his first collection of personal essays, *Eating Lightbulbs*, which deals with mental illness, poetry, and movies. He lives with his husband in Western New York.

Forrest Gander, born in the Mojave Desert, lives in California. A translator/writer with degrees in geology and literature, he's received the Pulitzer Prize and Best Translated Book Award, among many other honors. Gander's has been a signal voice for environmental poetics. His book *Twice Alive* focuses on human and ecological intimacies. In 2024, New Directions brought out his long poem on the desert, *Mojave Ghost: A Novel Poem.*

Jane Hirshfield: Writing "some of the most important poetry in the world today" (*The New York Times Magazine*), Jane Hirshfield is the author most recently of *The Asking: New & Selected Poems* (Knopf, 2023); two collections of essays; and four books collecting and co-translating world poets from the deep past. Hirshfield's honors include the Poetry Center Book Award, the California Book Award, and finalist selection for the National Book Critics Circle Award. Translated into seventeen languages, Hirshfield is a former chancellor of the Academy of American Poets and an elected member of the American Academy of Arts & Sciences.

Ilya Kaminsky is the author of critically acclaimed collections of poetry, *Dancing in Odesa* (2004) and *Deaf Republic* (2019). Both books were written in English, Kaminsky's second language. Over the years, Kaminsky has also become known for his passionate advocacy of translation of international literature in the United States. A long time poetry editor at *Words Without Borders*, and *Poetry International*, he has also edited several anthologies of poetry from around the world, including *Ecco Anthology of International Poetry* (HarperCollins), which is widely used in classrooms all over the country. He has also founded and edited Poets in the World, a book series which is dedicated to publishing compilations of poetry from around the globe, including places such as Iraq, China, Eastern Europe, South America, and elsewhere. He has also edited and translated several collections of poetry from Ukraine.

Danusha Laméris' third book of poems, *Blade by Blade*, was published by Copper Canyon Press in 2024. She is also the author of *The Moons of August*, winner of the Autumn House Press Poetry Prize, 2014, and *Bonfire Opera* (Pitt Poetry Series, 2020), finalist for the Paterson Poetry Prize and winner of the 2021 Northern California Book Award. Laméris is on the faculty of Pacific University's Low-Residency MFA program and lives in Santa Cruz, California. http://www.danushalameris.com

David Lehman's most recent books are *The Morning Line* (Pittsburgh UP), a gathering of poems, and *The Mysterious Romance of Murder: Crime, Detection, and the Spirit of Noir* (Cornell University Press). Of *The Mysterious Romance of Murder*, Lois Potter in London's *TLS* writes: "How often does a critical book actually make one want to read the books it discusses?" Lehman is the editor of *The Oxford Book of American Poetry*, series editor of *The Best American Poetry*, and a contributing editor of *The American Scholar*.

Phillip Lopate is the author of 20 books of poetry, fiction and nonfiction, including his latest, *A Year and a Day* and *My Affair with Art House Cinema*.

Denise Low, the former Kansas Poet Laureate, is author of *House of Grace, House of Blood* from the University of Arizona. Her other books include the memoir *The Turtle's Beating Heart: One Family's Story of Lenape Survival* (University of Nebraska Press), *Jigsaw Puzzling: Essays* (Meadowlark Press, Coffin Award), and *Casino Bestiary: Poems* (Spartan Press). Low is a founding board member of Indigenous Nations Poets (In-Na-Po) and former board member and board president of the Associated Writing Programs. Low taught at Haskell Indian Nations University, where she founded the creative writing program. She is a literary programmer for The 222, an arts organization in northern California.

Mary Mackey, author of *The Jaguars That Prowl Our Dreams: New and Selected Poems 1974 to 2018*, winner of the 2019 Eric Hoffer Award for the Best Book Published by a Small Press, a CIIS Women's Spirituality Book Award. Other books: *The Village of Bones: Sabalah's Tale*, a novel about Prehistoric Europe, plus 7 other collections of poetry and 13 other novels. Her latest book *Creativity: Where Poems Begin* is a nonfiction look at the origins of inspiration. Join my mailing list at http://eepurl.com/CrLHT More information at https://marymackey.com/

Charles A. Matz: University of Notre Dame, USA, La Sorbonne, University of Paris, France, Columbia University, USA, Iconographer for Washington National Cathedral, Chevalier del Légion d'Honneur de France.

Sandy McIntosh was born in Rockville Centre, New York, and received a BA from Southampton College, an MFA from Columbia University, and PhD from the Union Institute and University. His journalism has been published widely in *The New York Times, The New York Daily News, The Daily Beast, Newsday* and elsewhere. He has published sixteen volumes of poetry and prose. His collaboration with Denise Duhamel was published in *The Best American Poetry* online. He was awarded a Silver Medal for a film script in the Film Festival of the Americas and received a fellowship to The John Steinbeck Memorial Library Studio, Southampton College. For ten years, he was Managing Editor of *Confrontation,* Long Island University's national literary journal. He has been Executive Editor and Publisher of Marsh Hawk Press, Inc. for twenty-two years.

Stephen Paul Miller is the author of eight books of poetry including the forthcoming *Beautiful Snacks* (Marsh Hawk Press); the title poem of that book will appear in *Best American Poetry 2023*. His critical books include *The Seventies Now* (Duke UP) and the forthcoming *The Other New Deal: 1938-1945*. Miller was a Senior Fulbright Scholar at Jagiellonian University in Krakow, Poland, and he is a Professor of English at St. John's University in New York City.

Rusty Morrison is co-publisher of *Omnidawn* (www.omnidawn.com). Her latest book, *RISK,* was published this spring by Black Ocean. Her books include *After Urgency* (won Tupelo's Dorset Prize) & *the true keeps calm biding its story* (won Ahsahta's Sawtooth Prize, Laughlin Award, N.California Book Award, & DiCastagnola). She's a recipient of Civitella Ranieri's fellowship, UC Berkeley Art Research Center's Poetry & the Senses Program, and a recipient of other artist retreat fellowships. She gives writing consultations. Website: www.rustymorrison.com

Jim Natal is the author of the forthcoming collection *Everything Changes Everything,* the new chapbook *Étude in the Form of a Crow,* and five full-length poetry books including *Spare Room: Haibun Variations* and *Memory and Rain.* His work has appeared widely in journals and anthologies. A multi-year Pushcart Prize nominee, he served as curator and host of the long-running Literary Southwest Series, and is co-founder of indie publisher Conflux Press in Los Angeles.

Xiaoqiu Qiu is a poet from Tongxiang, China. His poetry collection *Other Side of Ocean* won the 2024 Marsh Hawk Poetry Prize. His work has been published in the *Gulf Coast Journal, Colorado Review, Los Angeles Review* and elsewhere. Currently, he is a Black Mountain Institute PhD Fellow at UNLV.

Spencer Rumsey is a professional editor, writer and author of his debut novel, *Kathmandu Rising.*

R.L. Stine is one of the best-selling children's authors in history. His *Goosebumps* and *Fear Street* book series have sold more than 400 million copies around the world and have been adapted for movies and TV. He lives in New York City with his wife Jane, a former editor and publisher. His newest title is: *Goosebumps House of Shivers: Say My Name, Say My Name!*

David St. John has been received The Rome Fellowship and The Award in Literature, both from The American Academy of Arts and Letters; the O. B. Hardison Prize from The Folger Shakespeare Library; and the George Drury Smith Lifetime Achievement Award. He is the author of many collections of poetry, most recently, *Prayer For My Daughter*, as well as a prose collection entitled *Where the Angels Come Toward Us*. David St. John has written two libretti: for the opera based on his book, *The Face*, by Donald Crockett, and the choral symphony, *The Shore*, by Frank Ticheli. He was also co-editor of *American Hybrid: A Norton Anthology of New Poetry*. A past chancellor of the Academy of American Poets and a member of the American Academy of Arts and Sciences, David St. John is a University Professor of English and Comparative Literature at the University of Southern California.

Liane Strauss is the author of four books of poetry and writes the monthly Substack *How to Read a Poem: A Love Story*. Her most recent collection, *The Flaws in the Story*, was chosen by Mary Jo Bang as the winner of the 2023 Marsh Hawk Press Poetry Prize.

Eileen R. Tabios has released over 60 collections of poetry, fiction, essays, and experimental biographies from publishers in 10 countries and cyberspace. She invented the hay(na)ku, a 21st century diasporic poetic form, and the MDR Poetry Generator that can create poems totaling theoretical infinity. Translated into languages, she also has edited, co-edited or conceptualized 15 anthologies. More information is at http://eileenrtabios.com

Susan Terris is a freelance editor and the author of 8 books of poetry, 17 chapbooks, 3 artist's books, and 2 plays. Her recent books are: *Green Leaves, Unseeing* (Marsh Hawk Press), *Dream Fragments* (Swan Scythe Press: Winner) 2020, *Familiar Tense* (Marsh Hawk) 2019, *Take Two: Film Studies* (Omnidawn) 2017,

Memos (Omnidawn) 2015; and *Ghost of Yesterday: New & Selected Poems* (Marsh Hawk) 2012. Journals include *The Southern Review, Georgia Review, Prairie Schooner, Beloit Poetry Journal, Blackbird,* and *Ploughshares.* Poems of hers have appeared in *Pushcart Prize* and *Best American Poetry.* Ms. Terris selected, arranged, and edited *Quest: A Writer's Journey* and also edited the 2022 Marsh Hawk Press volume *On Becoming A Poet.* She is editor emerita of *Spillway Magazine* and a poetry editor at *Pedestal.* www.susanterris.com

Amber Flora Thomas is the author of *Eye of Water,* which won the Cave Canem Poetry Prize for a first book by an African American poet. Her other books are *The Rabbits Could Sing,* and most recently, *Red Channel in the Rupture.* A recipient of the Dylan Thomas American Poet Prize, the Richard Peterson Poetry Prize, and the Ann Stanford Poetry Prize, her poetry and essays have been published, or are forthcoming in *The Georgia Review, Orion Magazine, Colorado Review, Alaska Quarterly Review, Ecotone,* and *Tin House,* as well as numerous other journals and anthologies. A native of northern California, she currently lives on the Pamlico River in North Carolina and teaches creative writing at East Carolina University.

Tony Trigilio's newest book is *Craft: A Memoir* (Marsh Hawk Press, 2023). His recent books of poetry are *Proof Something Happened,* selected by Susan Howe as the winner of the 2020 Marsh Hawk Press Poetry Prize (2021), and *Ghosts of the Upper Floor* (BlazeVOX [books] 2019). A volume of his selected poems, *Fuera del Taller del Cosmos,* was published in 2018 by Guatemala's Editorial Poe (translated by Bony Hernández). He is a Professor of English and Creative Writing at Columbia College Chicago.

New Titles in the Chapter One Series

From Marsh Hawk Press

On Becoming a Poet: Twenty-five Original Essays and Interviews

SUSAN TERRIS, EDITOR · SANDY MCINTOSH, SERIES EDITOR

Original memoirs by outstanding poets from diverse backgrounds who recall how they found their beginnings. While university creative writing programs generally seek to develop the talents of maturing writers, essential information about the development of the craft will be found in these early memoirs. Full page starred review in *Publishers Weekly*. Selected by *Poets & Writers* for their "Writer's Bookshelf." "Simply the best collection of essays I've ever read about the urgencies, accidents, experiences, and desires that allow people to emerge as the writers they had never dreamt they might become." —David St. John

The Inventor: A Poet's Transcolonial Autobiography

EILEEN R. TABIOS

From the author, a prolific poet, on creating unique and original poetic forms: "I wrote *The Inventor* not because it's about my life but, because it's an autobiography that connects history, language, and poetry in a unique way beyond narratives. I learned English because it became widespread in my birth land, the Philippines, through U.S. colonialism. That caused me, as a young poet, to feel estranged from my raw material: English. My poetry practice, however, would lift me out of politics to meet poetry more directly as its own type of language. Ultimately, my prolonged engagement with poets, enabled me to create poetry inventions that metaphorically disrupts colonialism by generating communities of readers and writers worldwide. These inventions include the "hay(na)ku" which has spread globally among poets and, most recently, the "Flooid" whose pre-writing condition precedent of a "good deed" makes poetry live redemptively and beyond the page. In *The Inventor*, I show how Poetry is not mere words but a proactive approach to improving our relationships with each other and life on our planet."

The Birth of The Best

BY DAVID LEHMAN

Every September, a new edition of *The Best American Poetry* appears, quickening pulses, provoking arguments. From one year to the next, the editor's name on the cover is different, as is the cover art. The series editor is the one constant. It is the title David Lehman has held since the inaugural volume came out in 1988.

The first chapter, written for the 2018 reissue of the inaugural volume of the series, gives an account of the birth of *The Best American Poetry* and is followed by the forewords Lehman wrote for the books that appeared in consecutive years from 2015 through 2022—years marked by the Trump presidency, the Covid pandemic, the pollution of civic discourse by way of social media, new forms of censorship, and now, Russia's invasion of Ukraine. Naturally, these developments have had a profound impact on the anthology's poets and their aims in their work. This book chronicles that history and, at the same time, serves as a personal introduction for editors beginning their own magazines, book series or small presses.

Creativity: Where Poems Begin

BY MARY MACKEY

What is creativity? Where do writers get their ideas? In this brilliantly written, profound, deeply personal examination of how creative ideas have come to her, award-winning poet and *New York Times* best-selling novelist Mary Mackey looks at the origins of inspiration, taking us to on a journey to the place where poetry begins. "Her quest makes *Creativity* a book for anyone who wants to understand how bursts of insight come not only to poets and writers but to all of us." —Mara Lynn Keller, PhD, Professor Emerita of Philosophy and Religion and Women's Studies, California

Plan B: A Poet's Survivors Manual

BY SANDY MCINTOSH

You need a *Plan B* if you want to put food on the table, wear shoes without holes in the soles, and stop living with roommates before you turn sixty. Taking us on a witty, fascinating, no-holds barred romp through his own experiences in the world of commercial writing and publishing, McIntosh reassures us that it is possible to have a successful career as a poet while holding down day jobs that make us better writers. "*Plan B*: is a wonderful book, an important book, a book aspiring writers of fiction and poetry should read." —David Lehman, Editor, *The Oxford Book of American Poetry*. Series Editor, *The Best American Poetry*

Craft: A Memoir

BY TONY TRIGILIO

An exploration of the writer's craft through a series of short, linked personal essays. Each chapter features an anecdote from the author's development as a writer that illustrates craft elements central to his body of work. *Craft: A Memoir* is an effort to understand craft through discussions of the direct experience of writing itself, through stories of how Trigilio became a writer. Whether discussing traditional or unconventional craft elements, each essay pivots on the idea that the most effective way to learn one's craft is through storytelling rather than the linear, business-memo pragmatism of how-to handbooks.

Where Did Poetry Come From: Some Early Encounters

BY GEOFFREY O'BRIEN

A memoir in episodes of some early encounters—with the spoken word, the written word, the sung word—in childhood and adolescence, encounters that suggested different aspects of the mysterious and shapeshifting phenomenon imperfectly represented by the abstract noun "poetry." From nursery rhymes and television theme songs, show tunes and advertising jingles, *Classic Comics* and Bible verses, to first meetings with the poetry of Stevenson, Poe, Coleridge, Ginsberg, and others, it tracks not final assessments but a description of the unexpected revelations that began to convey how poetry "made its presence known before it had been given a name."

Titles From Marsh Hawk Press

Jane Augustine *Arbor Vitae; Krazy; Night Lights; A Woman's Guide to Mountain Climbing*

Tom Beckett *~~Dipstick~~ (Diptych)*

William Benton *Light on Water*

Sigman Byrd *Under the Wanderer's Star*

Patricia Carlin: *Original Green; Quantum Jitters; Second Nature*

Claudia Carlson *The Elephant House; My Chocolate Sarcophagus; Pocket Park*

Lorna Dee Cervantes: *April on Olymbia*

Meredith Cole *Miniatures*

Jon Curley *The Installation of Fear; Hybrid Moments; Scorch Marks; Remnant Halo*

Joanne D. Dwyer *RASA*

Neil de la Flor *Almost Dorothy; An Elephant's Memory of Blizzards*

Chard deNiord *Sharp Golden Thorn*

Sharon Dolin *Serious Pink*

Joanne Dominique Dwyer *Rasa*

Steve Fellner *Blind Date with Cavafy; The Weary World Rejoices*

Thomas Fink *Zeugma, Selected Poems & Poetic Series; Joyride; Peace Conference; Clarity and Other Poems; After Taxes; Gossip*

Thomas Fink and Maya D. Mason *A Pageant for Every Addiction*

Norman Finkelstein *Inside the Ghost Factory; Passing Over*

Edward Foster *A Looking-Glass for Traytors; The Beginning of Sorrows; Dire Straits; Mahrem: Things Men Should Do for Men; Sewing the Wind; What He Ought to Know*

Paolo Javier *The Feeling is Actual*

Burt Kimmelman *Abandoned Angel; Somehow; Steeple at Sunrise; Zero Point Poiesis;* with Fred Caruso *The Pond at Cape May Point*

Basil King *Disparate Beasts: Part Two; 77 Beasts; Disparate Beasts; Mirage; The Spoken Word / The Painted Hand from Learning to Draw / A History*

Martha King *Imperfect Fit*

David Lehman *The Birth of* The Best

Phillip Lopate *At the End of the Day*

Mary Mackey *Breaking the Fever; The Jaguars That Prowl Our Dreams; Sugar Zone; Travelers With No Ticket Home; Creativity*

Jason McCall *Dear Hero*

Sandy McIntosh *The After-Death History of My Mother; Between Earth and Sky; Cemetery Chess; Ernesta, in the Style of the Flamenco; Forty-Nine Guaranteed Ways to Escape Death; A Hole In the Ocean; Lesser Lights; Obsessional; Plan B:*

Stephen Paul Miller *Any Lie You Tell Will Be the Truth; The Bee Flies in May; Fort Dad; Skinny Eighth Avenue; There's Only One God and You're Not It*

Daniel Morris *Blue Poles; Bryce Passage; Hit Play; If Not for the Courage*

Gail Newman *Blood Memory*

Geoffrey O'Brien *Where Did Poetry Come From; The Blue Hill*

Sharon Olinka *The Good City*

Christina Olivares *No Map of the Earth Includes Stars*

Justin Petropoulos *Eminent Domain*

Paul Pines *Charlotte Songs; Divine Madness; Gathering Sparks; Last Call at the Tin Palace*

Jacquelyn Pope *Watermark*

George Quasha *Things Done for Themselves*

Karin Randolph *Either She Was*

Rochelle Ratner *Balancing Acts; Ben Casey Days; House and Home*

Michael Rerick *In Ways Impossible to Fold*

Corrine Robins *Facing It; One Thousand Years; Today's Menu*

Liane Strauss *The Flaws in the Story*

Eileen R. Tabios *The Inventor: A Poet's Transcolonial Autobiography; Because I Love You I Become War; The Connoisseur of Alleys; I Take Thee, English, for My Beloved; The In(ter)vention of the Hay(na)ku; The Light Sang as It Left Your Eyes; Reproductions of the Empty Flagpole; Sun Stigmata; The Thorn Rosary* with j/j hastain *The Relational Elations of Orphaned Algebra*

Tony Trigilio: *Proof Something Happened; Craft: A Memoir*

Susan Terris *Green Leaves Unseeing; Familiar Tense; Ghost of Yesterday; Natural Defenses*

Lynne Thompson *Fretwork*

Madeline Tiger *Birds of Sorrow and Joy*

Tana Jean Welch *Latest Volcano*

Harriet Zinnes: *Drawing on the Wall; Light Light or the Curvature of the Earth; New and Selected Poems; Weather is Whether; Whither Nonstopping*

Xiaoqiu Qiu: *Other Side of Ocean* (anthology) *On Becoming a Poet*

YEAR	AUTHOR	TITLE	JUDGE
2004	Jacquelyn Pope	*Watermark*	Marie Ponsot
2005	Sigman Byrd	*Under the Wanderer's Star*	Gerald Stern
2006	Steve Fellner	*Blind Date with Cavafy*	Denise Duhamel
2007	Karin Randolph	*Either She Was*	David Shapiro
2008	Michael Rerick	*In Ways Impossible to Fold*	Thylias Moss
2009	Neil de la Flor	*Almost Dorothy*	Forrest Gander
2010	Justin Petropoulos	*Eminent Domain*	Anne Waldman
2011	Meredith Cole	*Miniatures*	Alicia Ostriker
2012	Jason McCall	*Dear Hero,*	Cornelius Eady
2013	Tom Beckett	*~~Dipstick~~ (Diptych)*	Charles Bernstein
2014	Christina Olivares	*No Map of the Earth Includes Stars*	Brenda Hillman
2015	Tana Jean Welch	*Latest Volcano*	Stephanie Strickland
2016	Robert Gibb	*After*	Mark Doty
2017	Geoffrey O'Brien	*The Blue Hill*	Meena Alexander
2018	Lynne Thompson	*Fretwork*	Jane Hirshfield
2019	Gail Newman	*Blood Memory*	Marge Piercy
2020	Tony Trigilio	*Proof Something Happened*	Susan Howe
2021	Joanne D. Dwyer	*Rasa*	David Lehman
2022	Brian Cochran	*Translation Zone*	John Yau
2023	Liane Strauss	*The Flaws in the Story*	Mary Jo Bang
2024	Xiaoqiu Qiu	*Other Side of Ocean*	John Keene